To Lee & G,
Thanks so much for all your help, prayers, & support in getting this book printed. I love you so much! Thanks for being such wonderful friends!
Love you!
Kim

Unless otherwise indicated, Scripture versus are marked from *Life Application Bible*: New International Version® Copyright © 1991. All rights reserved. Used by permission.

Cover by Nadia Komarowski, Marco Island, FL

## Heaven's Postcards

Copyright © 2009 by Kim Todd

Published by: ZMH Publishers, Inc. 7550 Mission Hills Drive #306-102 Naples, FL 34119-9603

www.zmhpublishers.com

Library of Congress Cataloging-in-Publication Data

Heaven's Postcards / Kim Todd

p. cm.

Includes bibliographical references.

ISBN-13: 978-0-615-28475-0

ISBN-10: 0615284752

**All rights reserved.** No part of this publication may be reproduced, stored in a retrieval system, or transmitted in any form or by any means- electronic, mechanical, digital, photocopy, recording, or any other— except for brief quotations in printed reviews, without the prior permission of the publisher.

**Printed in the United States of America.**

# HEAVEN'S POST CARDS

The true story of a young man's death

and the amazing miracles that followed

### Kim Todd

ZMH Publishers, Inc.

Naples, FL

THIS BOOK IS DEDICATED

TO THE LOVING MEMORY OF MY SON,

# ZACH EDWARD CRUISE

10/26/82 - 12/1/07

For the word of God is living and active

Hebrews 4:12 (niv)

# **DEATH...** It is something that will affect 100% of us. Quite a staggering statistic, wouldn't you say? Hmmm, not too many things can compare to that--100%. We **all** will experience death either by the loss of someone we love or it may be our own. No matter what, we will not escape it. Yet we live as if death couldn't happen to us.

Many people get confused about the author of death. They often blame God. Actually the devil is the author of death. God is the giver of life. God is the one who conquered death. God loves us more than we love our own children. He wants to lavish us with His love. But we have to accept it first. He doesn't force himself on us. He gave each of us our own free will.

I was guilty of thinking death could never happen to me or my family. It only happens to other people, but not us. That changed when my twenty five year old son, Zach was killed in a car accident December 1, 2007. From that moment on, my entire life changed.

As I write this, it has been a little over a year since he passed away. I have experienced so many unusual things and learned so much. Perhaps the "unusual" things have always been there to experience, but "life" just kept getting in the way. I never "stopped". I was always in a hurry and always so busy. When my son died, my life stopped. I had never felt so much pain and it went so deep. The roller coaster of emotions was overwhelming. I wasn't sure if I would ever be able to take another breath, much less continue on with my life. But God was faithful in his love for me. He proved to me very loud and clear that He controls the universe.

As I sat down to write the outline of my story for this book, I was astonished at all that has happened in the past year. If I had not experienced it myself, I'm not sure I would have believed all this could happen to one family. I assure you, everything that is written within these pages is true.[1] Most of the events occurred with witnesses or we were able to take pictures as proof. I am so amazed at the depth of God's love for us.

I had always believed in God and in Heaven. But I was still a little afraid of the "unknown". Now I am so excited to go to Heaven. Who wouldn't want to go to a place where there is no heartache, pain, hunger, crime, or death….? God's promises are real. I encourage you to stop and check it out.

Psalm 19:1-4 (niv[2]) *"The heavens declare the glory of God; the skies proclaim the work of his hands. Day after day they pour forth speech; night after night they display*

---

[1] Names have been changed
[2] All quoted NIV text has been reprinted from *Holy Bible New International Version Concordance* Copyright 1982, 1984 by Zondervan Corporation Grand Rapids, MI 49530

*knowledge. There is no speech or language where their voice is not heard. Their voice goes out into all the earth, their words to the ends of the world."*

Romans: 6:23 (niv)   *"For the wages of sin is death, but the gift of God is eternal life in Christ Jesus our Lord."*

ASK, BELIEVE, RECEIVE……..

<u>Ask</u> for your sins to be forgiven, <u>Believe</u> Christ died for your sins, <u>Receive</u> eternal life

<u>Ask</u> God for Help, <u>Believe</u> God hears your prayer, <u>Receive</u> a blessing beyond anything you can imagine

## **MY FAMILY**

My parents divorced when I was seven years old. My mom moved in with her parents in order to raise her three children in a Christian home. She tried to shelter us from "the world" as much as possible.

When I was a young teenager I told God I was tired of my mundane "Christian" life. I felt like we lived in the dark ages. Even though my mom did her best to give us everything we needed, I was bored. There is a big world out there and my restless spirit longed for something more. I told God I wanted to experience some adventure. Let me tell you folks….be careful what you pray for. God actually hears your prayers.

It didn't take long for everything in my life to change.

Four of my friends died within four months as a result of automobile accidents. I did not understand it. How could God let people who had their entire lives ahead of them die so young? It didn't make sense to me. Why? Why??? How could God be so cruel?

Death is so final. My friends didn't have a chance to live their lives yet.

After my friends died, I started drifting away from God. I thought he was cruel and was afraid of him. I kept thinking what if that had been me. I didn't want to die at a young age; it would be such a waste. I had not accomplished or experienced much in my life.

I moved away from my family when I was eighteen. I was very head strong and married a man I had only known for six weeks. He offered adventure and excitement, just what I was looking for in my life. We traveled all over the United States for a while and finally settled in Florida.

We were married for five years when our beautiful son, Zach was born. His birth was the most awesome thing I had ever experienced. I never knew you could love someone so much. He was so innocent, so helpless, and totally dependent on me. It scared me to death.

I marveled at the miracle of life. It made me very proud. I wanted to make sure I did everything right for my baby. I vowed to be there for my child no matter what he encountered in this world. My child *will* have a good and happy life.

I decided to start going to church again now that I had a child. Raising children in a Christian home would help them be prepared to battle the trials life will throw at them. Besides I knew it was the right thing to do. My husband scoffed at me. He thought church was for weak people, so Zach and I went alone.

Three years later God blessed me with a darling daughter, Haven. She was so cute and tiny. She was a little baby doll to me. I was worried that Zach would be jealous of her at first, but he adored her. He was so sweet and nurturing towards her. Everything was perfect except one thing. My husband was an alcoholic and my marriage was terrible.

I tried to make the best of my marriage but eleven years had gone by and I'd had enough. I wanted to leave my husband. I decided to keep a diary.

My family lived eight hundred and fifty miles away. I hid the diary at my mother's house during my last visit. I planned to have mom read it later. Maybe she would make sense out of all this. Was my bad marriage really my fault? My husband sure thought it was. I need someone to help me do the right thing. I knew the bible said you should not divorce your husband but surely there was a loop hole in there somewhere. One thing was for certain, my mom sure knew the bible!

After I returned home, I finally summed up enough courage to swallow my pride and call my mom. I told her I had some problems and needed to talk to her. I explained I had left the journal and asked her to read it. I wanted her to tell me what I should do.

I didn't quite get the response I had expected. She responded by saying she didn't want to read it that she would worry about me. She said I should 'take it to the Lord in prayer'.

I could not believe my ears. I thought, "What? This is my mother! 'Take it to the Lord in prayer'! Gosh mom I need someone to TELL me what to do. You're *still* living in the dark ages! I can't *hear* God's voice! Don't you know He *doesn't talk*?"

Her advice ended up being the best thing she could have done for me. It forced me to depend on God. I had no one to tell me what to do. I didn't want to talk to my friends, nor the people at my church. I was afraid they would judge me. I had no other place to go for advice.

I cried for hours and I felt so hopeless. Knowing I had no other recourse, I finally said, "OK God, if you are real let me hear your voice. Tell me what to do." I waited for a voice to thunder down but heard nothing. I kept begging and praying, "I really do need you Lord. Please help me."

Weeks passed, I didn't hear a voice or have a clear answer but inside I felt calmer. I kept praying. Any kind of relief was better than the torment I had been experiencing. Finally, late one night I got my answer. Something happened and it was *very* clear I had to leave my husband.

Psalms 37:7 (niv) *"Be still before the Lord and wait patiently for him."*

The church I had attended fell apart shortly before I left my husband. I quit my job at a construction company where I had worked for the past ten years. I moved into a trailer park with my two children and tried to disappear from the life I left behind. Nothing was the same. All aspects of my life were changing. I was glad. I didn't like where I had been. The only good thing from my past was my two beautiful children.

Weeks had passed since I began my new life. It was time to start looking for a job. I was hired right away by a Construction Company. It was a father and son business. I fell in love with the father, Ron. He was so kind and full of compassion. Everyone who came in contact with Ron always left with a smile. He helped me in so many ways and made me feel like a worthy person. I was so beaten and insecure from my past experiences.

Ron shared many stories of the trials he overcame in his life. He told stories how God had helped him. He said the Bible was the "Living Word" and all of life's answers were in there. He and his wife asked me to go to church with them. I loved their church and started going regularly with my children.

My job didn't last very long with Ron and his son. They needed someone with an accounting degree which I did not have. The son broke the news to me but offered to let me stay until I got a new job. I was devastated. What was I going to do now? Yesterday, I felt like everything was going in the right direction for me and my children. It was the first time I had felt good about my life since I moved away from North Carolina. Today, I felt like all hope was gone for a good future. I felt so alone and scared.

Ron came in while I was sitting on the floor filing papers in the bottom drawer of a file cabinet. I was still in shock. He sat down on the floor beside me. I felt a lump in my throat and could not speak. He reached over and hugged me. We cried like two babies. Not a word was said. We cried until there were no more tears. I didn't want him to let me go. It was the first hug I had had in a long time. It was so foreign to me and it felt so good. I didn't know a hug could say so much.

For years I had made a point to keep my distance from all men but this man was different. He had a purity that set him apart from all other men. This man changed my life. He told me no matter how bad life gets, you have to keep pushing forward. Never give up.

I felt like Ron was one of God's angels sent here to help me. He encouraged me to put one foot forward. After all, you can't get anywhere by standing still. You have to put yourself in motion. Ron helped me believe God *does* take care of us if we let him.

I finally had to leave Ron's company. They hired my replacement and I couldn't stay any longer. I looked everywhere for a job but there was none available. Months passed and I was getting frantic. I borrowed money from my credit cards to buy groceries, pay rent, and pay my bills. I was getting seventy five dollars a week for child support which barely paid the care for both children while I looked for work. I prayed and asked God to help me. I *really* needed to hear his voice. Oh how I wished God could talk.

I was pacing the floor one night and I looked at my bible. I picked it up and told God I *needed* to *know* he could hear me. Ron had referred to the bible as "the Living Word". I had heard other people say it too. I hugged the bible to my chest and cried frantically. I asked God to make it talk to me.

As I was asking God to talk to me, a thought popped into my head…. 'Open your bible'. I sort of laughed at myself, thinking, "Yes that would help wouldn't it!" I opened my bible and the first thing I saw were the words "**Do Not Worry**". It was the heading for Matthew 6:25,26 (niv) *"Therefore I tell you, do not worry about your life, what you will eat or drink, or about your body, what you will wear. Is not life more important than food, and the body more important than clothes? Look at the birds of the air, they do not sow or reap or store away in barns, and yet your heavenly Father feeds them. Are you not much more valuable than they?"*

I could not believe what I had read. Talk about hitting the topic right on the head! Maybe there *is* something about this "Living Word" stuff! I felt all giddy inside. I thanked God for this clear message. I wasn't sure if it was a coincidence or not. But I felt like a little kid! I was awestruck and told God I *would* trust him. I'd let him take care of *everything* for me. Somehow, I knew He would. I went to bed that night feeling elated. I felt like a little child waiting for Christmas to arrive.

The next day around 10:00 my phone rang. It was a construction company I had interviewed with several times in the past couple of months. They offered me a job and asked me to come in to work out the details. I was so excited when I hung up the phone. I was laughing as I looked up towards the ceiling and said "Boy you're fast!! Thank you."

Within a few minutes the phone rang again. It was *another* construction company calling to offer me a job! They too wanted me to come in to work out the details. I set a time and hung up. I looked at the ceiling again and shook my head in amazement. "Man, you're something God. Two job offers within five minutes of each other after I had been trying for months to get *just* one. *Now* you have to tell me *which one* I should choose!!!" I started laughing like a little kid on a play ground. I laughed and giggled as tears of joy streamed down my face. Wow, God *is* real. He actually *does* talk!

This was the beginning of my personal relationship with God. He became my best friend and has proven His love and faithfulness to me and my family over and over through the years.

Months later my future husband, Steve moved in next door to me. He had been through many trials himself. He had full custody of his daughter Monica. Steve's dream was to have a good wife and wonderful family life for his daughter. My dream was the same.

Over the years, God was very present in our life. He protected me from a stalker, an arsonist, and a man in a drunken rage that put a gun to my head. He healed my daughter when she was almost paralyzed from a minor operation where something went wrong. God saved my son in a horrific gun accident. He protected my husband when he fell off a two story scaffold, head first.[1] My family has been through some very unusual trials but through each one God provided miracles beyond anything we could have ever imagined. I was sure God had a shield of protection around me and my family. He would not let any harm come to us. He had proven that over and over again. God was my best friend.

Yep, I was SURE that God would not let anything happen to us. I just knew it.

John 9:3 (niv) " *'neither this man nor his parents sinned,' said Jesus, 'but this happened so that the work of God might be displayed in his life."*

## **THE ACCIDENT**

It was Friday night and everything was going so well. When I went to bed that night, I told my husband, Steve that I had never been happier. Everything was so perfect. In one week we were going on an eight day cruise to the Eastern Caribbean. We received a call earlier that day from the Cruise lines saying they were giving us a free upgrade to a Stateroom with a Balcony. The remaining jobs in our business would be completed by the end of next week. We can take off with no worries. I had just finished all my Christmas shopping which was a first. I had always dreamed of getting my shopping done early and I actually accomplished it this year! There was nothing that could stress me out now. I was ecstatic. Everything was so perfect.

But then my phone rang around 5:00 in the morning. It was the hospital telling us that my son, Zach was involved in a serious automobile accident. They said I should come to the hospital as soon as possible. The tone of the lady's voice did not sound very good. I asked her if Zach would be ok. She said, "it is very *very* serious."

Steve and I got dressed and he drove us to the hospital. I wanted to ensure my son would be ok so I called my Mom and our friends Jim and Mary to pray for Zach. I've seen prayer bring unbelievable miracles. I also called Dennis, Zach's dad. Not once did I think that Zach would not make it. I was sure he would be OK. God knows my children are my greatest joy. My whole life was lived for them.

When we arrived at the hospital, they told us Zach's neck was broken, his internal organs were badly damaged, and he had lost a lot of blood due to a main artery being severed. They gave him a five to ten percent chance of survival. I was *sure* he would survive. I told the nurse we've had miracles before, and he would make it. Please don't give up.

I remembered when Haven faced paralysis from a minor operation. The experience resulted in a miracle and two people came to know Christ through the ordeal. This was just another trial that we would get through somehow and marvel over later.

I didn't care how long it would take for Zach to recover. I *know* God never gives us more than we can handle and we would get through this. God wouldn't let my son die.

When they told me Zach did not make it, I thought they were lying. It couldn't be true. It wasn't until I saw him that I finally accepted the fact that he was really gone. I felt like God had betrayed me. I was in shock. This could *not* be happening to my family.

This was the worst thing any parent could go through. No matter what age your child, a parent feels the need to protect their children from this crazy world and care for them. When our children die before we do, we somehow feel responsible, like we have failed them. I felt so helpless. There was nothing I could do. I was afraid that Zach had not gone to heaven. He had never been baptized. I prayed for God to protect my baby. I begged God to help Zach not be afraid, to please take him directly into his arms.

God knew this is the ONLY thing that I couldn't handle. I adore my children, they were everything to me. I had told God this so many times.

But there was no miracle for this situation. My son, my beautiful baby, my pride and joy was gone. My pain was unbearable. It ran so deep that I could barely breathe from the ache inside of me. The pain was overwhelming.

I cried all day. I kept asking God why? How could he do this to me? I thought about how God must have felt when he lost his son. I asked Him if he felt this bad when his Son died. I knew God must have hurt as badly as I did and possibly more. His Son died a brutal death even though he was a good person who never hurt anyone. Then a bible verse popped into my head so clearly. It was the same verse that had given me peace when my daughter, Haven suffered her neck injury. The verse was *"All the days ordained for me were written in your book before one of them came to be."* Psalm 139:16b (NIV)

I asked God, was this *planned* all along? Is there a *reason* for Zach's death? How can anything *good* come out of this?

Jeremiah 1:5 (niv) *"Before I formed you in the womb, I knew you, before you were born, I set you apart."*

Later as I was curled up in my bed crying and begging God to help me understand, I kept seeing the words **"TRUST ME"** when I closed my eyes. The words were big and bold. I said to God, "I *do* trust you but I just don't understand". The only prayer I could utter was "God, I hurt".

Romans 8:26 (niv) *"in the same way, the Spirit helps us in our weakness. We do not know what we ought to pray for, but the Spirit himself intercedes for us with groans that words cannot express"*

Some things happen to us in this world that breaks our heart. The devil seizes the opportunity to enter the crack of our heart where it was broken. He keeps nagging at us and pushes us to confusion and makes us feel that everything is our fault. The devil makes us forget that God is in control of our life if we give our life to Him. ONLY GOD can control whether we live or die. God tells us this all through the Bible and He has proved it to me over and over.

Everything that happens in our life is for a reason. God tells us that He will never give us more than we can handle. Sometimes, I think He is mistaken about how much I can handle. But God is there with us and is taking care of us if we just call out to Him. Matthew 11:28-29 (niv) *"Come to me, all you who are weary and burdened, and I will give you rest. Take my yoke upon you and learn from me, for I am gentle and humble in heart, and you will find rest for your souls."*

Psalm 138:7-8 (niv) *"you reach out your hand, and the power of your right hand saves me. The Lord will work out his plans for my life for your faithful love, O Lord endures forever."*

God showed me He was there during Zach's death. He's been showing me in amazing ways ever since. I realize now God is using my son's death to save others. I didn't understand it at first, but now I do. The "signs" all started on the third day.

Hosea 6: 2b (niv) *"on the third day, He will restore us".*

Ps 147:3 (niv) *"he heals the brokenhearted and binds up their wounds"*

Psalms 42:5, 11 (niv) *"Why are you downcast, o my soul? Why so disturbed within me? Put our hope in God, for I will yet praise him, my Savior and my God."*

**THE WARNING**

Our friend, Warren came over shortly after Zach's death and told me to be careful and not turn away from God. I told him that would never happen. Didn't he know how much I love God? I didn't realize the devil was going to try to tear my family apart. But my friend did. He had lost his son fifteen years earlier and was trying to warn me.

Soon after Warren's visit, every single aspect of my life went haywire. Everyone seemed to get aggravated over little things. I ignored our finances to the point that checks started bouncing in our business and personal accounts. I got sick and was in bed for two weeks. We were involved in two totally unfounded lawsuits. I got so angry at a woman at church that I wanted to hit her, all because she acted happy during the worship songs. Everything and everyone around me was a mess. One day I got into a screaming match in my front yard with one of our employees. I could not believe I had done that. It was then I realized that the devil had gotten to us. Warren had been right. The devil *was* trying to turn us away from God and from giving Him glory in our situation. I contacted my closest friends and asked them to help me pray the devil away. It worked. I felt peace right away and within three days, I began to feel like everything would be ok.

God showed us many signs that Zach was in Heaven. He used the clouds, the stars, birds, butterflies, the radio, and words from friends. I was amazed at how clearly He spoke to us. He used the clouds to show us a perfect heart, a cross, an "I love you" sign, the word HI, and a hand writing the letters **Z a c** in the clouds. God used birds to hug us, wave at us, and do flips in the air at us. He used stars and butterflies to show He controls everything in our universe. He showed me things in the Bible that I had never seen before that gave me such peace. He used friends to tell me things or bring me books that enlightened me about questions I had. God's presence was everywhere.

In the first four months after Zach's death, seven people we knew died. Since then ten more people we know have died. I've met many people at the cemetery who recently lost someone they loved. I used to run *away* from people who were going through the loss of a loved one. But now I run *to* them. I want to share God's love and faithfulness with them. I want them to know that God is real. That He really is the same today, as He was yesterday, and He will be forever. God hasn't changed. He's always been there for us. He loves us no matter what.

I Peter 5:6-11 (niv) *"Humble yourselves, therefore, under God's mighty hand, that he may lift you up in due time. Cast all your anxiety on him because he cares for you. Be self-controlled and alert, Your enemy the devil prowls around like a roaring lion looking for someone to devour. Resist him, standing firm in the faith, because you know that your brothers throughout the world are undergoing the same kind of sufferings. And the God of all grace, who called you to his eternal glory in Christ, after you have suffered a little while, will himself restore you and make you strong, firm, and steadfast. To him be the power for ever and ever. Amen*

A few days after Zach's death we found a bible in his bedroom. He had marked a passage with a piece of paper. It read: Psalm 25:7 (niv) *"Remember not the sins of my youth and my rebellious ways; according to your love remember me for you are good, O Lord."*

**SIGNS**

**1 Corinthians 2:9-10 (niv)** "However it is written, 'no eye has seen, no ear has heard, no mind has conceived what God has prepared for those who love him' but God has revealed it to us by his Spirit."

1. Zach's House
2. Bumper Stickers
3. Survey Stakes
4. The Poem
5. The Funeral
6. Zach's Tattoo
7. Butterflies
8. Birds
9. Stars
10. Broken Neck
11. Clouds
12. Easter
13. The Radio
14. Only Son
15. Idols
16. Dreams
17. Cards/Books
18. Kayla's Toast
19. Raybo
20. Thoughts

### Zach's House

Dennis, Steve, and I went to Zach's house to get some clothes for Zach to wear at his funeral. Zach's step sister Monica wanted to make a DVD of his life and asked us to get some of his CDs to use on the video. When I walked into his house I could hardly breathe. I started crying so hard and wished that I could hold my son. Zach bought his own home when he was twenty one years old. He had had so many dreams that would never happen now. I could not believe this was real. I missed him so much. This was the first time I had ever been at his house that I didn't get a hug from him. I had always told him he was the best hugger in the whole world. He really was.

I went into his bedroom and walked around the room touching everything. It was exactly as he left it. I could almost feel his presence in the room. As I walked past his dresser, I noticed a Thesaurus that was lying on top. It was so white and bright, it was if it were glowing. I said, "Huh, a Thesaurus. I wonder why Zach has a Thesaurus." Then I continued walking around his room. I went through his clothes and we all agreed on what he should wear.

We started towards the front door to leave and I remembered that I needed to get some of Zach's CDs for Monica. I walked over to Zach's stereo and pushed the button to open the CD tray. The first thing I saw was a CD that read in big letters **"LIFE AFTER DEATH"**. Obviously I lost it again. I showed it to Dennis and Steve. We stood there discussing what just happened. I told them it was a sign that Zach is in Heaven, and he was trying to tell us that.

After discussing that thought with Dennis and Steve we started to leave again. I wanted to go into Zach's kitchen for a minute. We had been everywhere in his house but there. I just felt the need to go check it out. I walked into Zach's kitchen. Sitting in the sink by itself was a coffee cup. The words on the cup jumped at me. "**I SAID A PRAYER FOR YOU TODAY**". I couldn't believe it; the words were so big and tall. I picked it up and finished reading the rest of the cup. It read:

*I said a prayer for you today*
*And know God must have heard*
*I felt the answer in my heart*
*Although He spoke not a word*
*I didn't ask for wealth or fame (I knew you wouldn't mind)*
*I asked for priceless treasures of a more lasting kind...*
*I prayed that He'd be near you at the start of each new day*
*To grant you Health and Blessings, and friends to share your way*
*I asked for happiness for you, in all things great and small*
*And that you'd know His loving care, I prayed for most of all.*

Wow. I read it again to Dennis and Steve. God is allowing us to have signs that He *is* taking care of Zach. I love you God. Thank you. I started to feel such peace. I just knew Zach was in Heaven and that God *was* holding him and caring for him. God hadn't let me down!

Proverbs 3:5 (niv) *"Trust in the Lord with all your heart and lean not on your own understanding"*

I often say if you don't know the answer to something, pray about it and wait three days. God will give you a clear answer by then. All this happened in the first three days after my son's death. God was making it very clear that there *is* life after death.

The next day I told Jim, our friend and Pastor that I wanted tell this story at Zach's funeral. I don't do well speaking in front of people, but I just knew this was what God wanted me to do. Why else would he have given me the signs I just got. God wanted me to use Zach's death to help other people.

1 Timothy 4:6 (niv) *"If you point these things out to the brothers, you will be a good minister of Christ Jesus, brought up in the truths of the faith and of the good teaching that you have followed."*

**BUMPER STICKERS**

It was the morning of Zach's funeral. It had been six days since the accident. A lot had happened. I was still reeling over the events that had taken place. I knew God had a reason for Zach's death, but the "unknown" scared me. I just wanted to take care of my baby. God had been so faithful to leave me little signs that Zach was with him but I could not shake the feeling that I had let my son down.

We were on the way to the funeral home to view Zach's body before they transported him to the church. The service was to be held later that day. A few days earlier the funeral director had asked me to write a list of the pall bearers and give it to him. I had not written it yet. I started to write the names down on the way to the funeral home. My mind kept wandering back to the thought that I had let my son down. It was causing me to ache so deeply inside. I told Steve how I felt as I looked down at the empty paper. He told me I had been a great mother and there was nothing that I could have done differently. I sighed as I looked up and said, "There is nothing more I can do now".

Just as I had finished speaking the words, a car started to pass us. It had a bumper sticker that read "TEACH YOUR CHILDREN WELL". I laughed feebly and read it aloud to Steve. Then I sadly said, "I tried."

I looked down at the paper and started to write the names. A van passed us and I looked up. In the back window was a big decal that read, "SPIRIT TAXI". I half heartedly laughed again and pointed out to Steve. Then I said, "I wonder if this is another sign. I can't *wait* to see the *next* bumper sticker! " We continued our drive to the Funeral Home and I looked at every car around us, hoping for another sign. Not one car had a bumper sticker or any other signs of graffiti.

We were a few blocks from the funeral home and I told Steve I doubt we are going to get any more signs. We approached a stop light and I finished writing the pall bearers names. When I looked up a car pulled up beside me and made a right turn. As I looked at the car, it had a big bumper sticker that read, "PEACE WITHIN ME". I started giggling and laughing. "God really loves me. He is making sure that I know Zach is all right." Then I repeated all three bumper stickers: **TEACH YOUR CHILDREN WELL...SPIRIT TAXI... PEACE WITHIN ME** . God was letting me know that I had done all I could to protect my son. I had raised him to know and love God. God took him on a ride to heaven and now my son is experiencing such peace and joy.

Zach is experiencing a joy so great that we on earth can't *even begin* to imagine.

**Isaiah 25:8b (niv)** "The Lord has spoken, He will swallow up death forever. The Sovereign Lord will wipe away the tears from all faces."

## SURVEY STAKES

We arrived at the Funeral Home and I couldn't wait to tell Dennis and Haven about what had just happened. All of us had been dreading seeing Zach in his casket. Dennis and Haven had not seen Zach since they had found out he died. Dennis had always been a skeptic regarding life after death or anything to do with God.

When we pulled into the parking lot, Haven and Dennis were standing outside waiting for us. Dennis had a huge smile on his face and was showing something to Haven. It was not quite the reaction I was expecting especially since Dennis was very angry over Zach's death.

Zach worked as a surveyor for many years up until the company closed about eight weeks before his death. Dennis had been walking the beach that morning as he did almost every morning. He walked past a bench that was a memorial to a friend of his, Bobby who died years earlier. He looked at the memorial plaque and thought about Bobby's wife and son. He felt badly that he had not been supportive of them over the years. Death just made him very uncomfortable. He never knew what to say.

Dennis continued walking another block and was talking to Zach the whole way. He asked for a sign that he was ok. He then turned around to start back and when he did, he saw two survey stakes stuck in the ground. He almost freaked as he looked around to find more survey stakes. He could not find any. He knew that the stakes were not there when he walked past. He knew no one would believe him so he decided to take a picture of the stakes. He had never used the camera on his cell phone. He wished Zach was here to help him. Zach had always been very good with all the electronic stuff.

Dennis took the picture. He was not sure it took properly so he opened his phone to find it. When he opened his phone, the picture of the survey stakes appeared on the main screen as the wallpaper background. He had no idea how this could have happened but one thing for sure, he just got the sign he was asking for.

Dennis continued to walk the beach every day, looking for more survey stakes or even a surveyor. Over a week had passed and he finally saw a surveyor. He went up to him and asked him about the stakes. The man said he had no idea. They had been working further north of that area previously and there was no reason what so ever for survey stakes to be right there.

## **THE POEM**

I was lying in bed dreading Zach's funeral which was a few hours away. I was trying to be strong but I wasn't sure if I would make it through the funeral. We were having the viewing and then a service immediately after. It was almost time to go to the Church.

I was lying in bed unable to make myself move. I was asking God to help me through this as it was the most painful thing I had ever experienced. I thanked Him for the signs He had given us. I was praying for His continued peace for me and my family. I was still having trouble breathing and I was afraid I'd pass out. Steve came in the bedroom and was acting strangely. He said that Monica had found something that Zach had written and they weren't sure if they should show it to me.

The day before Monica asked if she could get something of Zach's as a keepsake. Steve, Monica, Haven, and I rode together to Zach's house later that night. While we were there, Monica saw the Thesaurus that I had seen a few days earlier. She asked if she could have it. I sort of laughed and said that it was perfect for her since she was the only one who would actually use it.

While waiting to leave for the funeral, Monica was sitting thinking about Zach and thumbing through his Thesaurus, where she found a poem he had written. She read it and then showed it to Steve. That's when he came into my room.

When Steve gave me the letter I thought someone was pulling a joke on me. The top of the letter was titled "If I Die 2nite". It was a poem that Zach had written on June 15, 07. He died December 1, 2007. It read:

**If I Die 2Nite**

**Mama Please don't cry**
**You know you've raised me right**
**And are always by my side**
**But I'm in a better place and time**
**Now that I've died**
**I've often seen my own demise**
**Quick and painless**
**Maybe it's for the best**
**Not growin old before I'm put to rest**
**Because ain't nothing worse than this cursed earth**
**Born and Bred to die since birth**
**So please Mama don't cry**
**This is your Son in the sky**
**Now sit back and watch me fly**

**Zach**

I could not believe it. A letter from the grave, how bazaar is that? I read it several more times and then I jumped out of bed. My Son really *is* in Heaven. God is telling me this loud and clear! I need to celebrate his life and assure all the people hurting that Zach *is* in Heaven.

This just reaffirms the bible verse that kept going through my mind since the first day of my son's death. **Psalm 139:16** *"All the days ordained for me were written in your book before one of them came to be."*

Matthew 5:4 (niv) *"Blessed are those who mourn, for they will be comforted"*

God's promises are real.

## **THE FUNERAL**

The funeral service was beautiful. I read a story I had written earlier about the coffee cup and CD. Then I told everyone about the Poem and read it too. I didn't cry during the whole thing. I know people thought I was on some really good drugs or something like that, but I don't like poisoning my body with drugs, alcohol, or other foreign items. I consider my body a gift from God and want to take care of it the best I can. Besides, if God had wanted to speak to me, I wanted to be coherent!

Over five hundred people attended the service. Zach's first cousin Chris stood up at the service and told a story about an adventure that he, Zach, and David had had. Chris had been devastated by the news of Zach's death. They were really close friends. They were six months apart in age and pretty much like two peas in a pod. They had done a lot of things together over the years. The first night after hearing the news, Chris was outside with his dog. He looked up at the stars and said "Alright Zach, where ya at?" As soon as he finished speaking a shooting star streaked across the sky. He then felt Zach's presence close to him. Chris said his dog was even wagging his tail at something, but nobody was there.

The next day after the grave side service, Chris walked away towards the mausoleum near Zach's grave. He started yelling at me, "Kim come here." I went over to him. He was smiling at me as he pointed to a plaque on the wall. He said "Look". I started reading the plaque and it read

> **PERHAPS THEY ARE NOT STARS IN THE SKY**
> **BUT RATHER OPENINGS WHERE OUR LOVED ONES SHINE DOWN**
> **TO LET US KNOW THEY ARE HAPPY**

Chris then started toward Zach's grave to thank him for the sign. He stopped again just before the grave and pointed to the ground, smiling. I looked at the plaque on a grave close to Zach's. All it said was "David", the same name as the friend in the story that Chris told at the funeral the night before.

A lot of people told me later that they had never felt such peace at a funeral. They were hesitant at first but then mentioned that it was truly the most beautiful funeral they had ever attended.

Isaiah 25:9 (niv) *"In that day they will say, "Surely this is our God; we trusted him, and he saved us. This is the Lord, we trusted him; let us rejoice and be glad in his salvation"*

**ZACH'S TATTOO**

When Zach was around ten years old, he started asking for a tattoo. I told him that I didn't like tattoos but if he really wanted one, he had to wait until he was eighteen. I would joke with him and tell him when he gets one it should read, 'I love my momma'. Even before he turned eighteen, Zach started searching for the right tattoo. He didn't get one right away. I had expected he would.

Six months after his eighteenth birthday and the week before Easter, Zach came home and told me he finally got a tattoo. I felt sick thinking, "Oh no, I hope it's not something he'll regret in later years." When he showed it to me, I was amazed. It was the most beautiful, detailed picture of praying hands that I had ever seen. I felt so proud. I told him honestly that it was beautiful. I was practically speechless.

On Easter Sunday, Zach was sitting on the couch with his shirt off, looking at something. I took a picture of his tattoo.

After Zach died, one thing that kept nagging at me was not being 100% sure that Zach was in Heaven. I kept getting signs that he was, but still there was an uneasy feeling about it. I knew he did not go to church and had not been living the "perfect" life. While he was in elementary and middle school he attended the

*A.W.A.N.A.* program at our church. He had made a proclamation of faith when he was twelve years old but had never been baptized. It kept nagging at me but I never said it. Was Zach really saved? I felt such regret that I didn't push him harder to go to church.

One day I was looking through the pictures Monica had taken from our photo albums to put on the DVD of Zach's life. The one I had taken of Zach's tattoo of the praying hands was in the group of pictures. I stared at the picture. It was the first time I had noticed there was red coming out of the center of the hands where they were clasped. It looked like blood flowing from where the nails pierced Christ's hands when he hung on the cross. It reminded me Christ died so our sins would be forgiven. It says it so clearly in John 3:16 *"for God so loved the world that He gave his only Son that whosoever **believes** in him shall not perish but have everlasting life"*. Nothing is said about living a perfect life. God made it so simple. Just believe. I knew Zach believed in God. We talked about God all the time.

I thought about John 3:16 again. It's amazing how you hear something so often that you become callous to it. You just don't stop to reflect on what it really means. I realized once you accept the gift of Salvation and God writes your name in the Book of Life, He doesn't erase it. God doesn't take back his gift of Salvation to us once we've accepted it. He's not an Indian giver.

God, you are so amazing. Why do you love us all so much?

Matthew 18:14 (niv) *"In the same way your Father in heaven is not willing that any of these little ones should be lost"*

## **BUTTERFLIES**

It was Saturday the day after the funeral and everyone was leaving town, including Steve and I to go on our cruise. Steve's dad and step mother were taking the cruise with us. We had planned this trip earlier in the year. His dad's health was bad. They had dreamed of taking a cruise with Steve and me before his dad became too sick to take one.

I felt guilty leaving, but everyone insisted that we should go as it would be good for me to get away. Our phone had been ringing off the hook and people were constantly stopping in, so this would give me a chance to reflect, rest, and talk to God. My Bible Study girls had gotten me a leather journal and they encouraged me to keep a log of my journey dealing with the loss of my son.

The week during the cruise, I spent a lot of time sleeping, eating, writing, and crying. I didn't want to do anything. I didn't feel like doing any of the shore excursions, so Steve, his dad, and step mother decided to take a tour of Antigua without me. After they left, I went down to the dining room for some food. I sat by myself overlooking the island in front of a large glass window. I was having trouble swallowing the food as it was still hard to eat anything. Suddenly, a beautiful yellow butterfly with brown spots flew up to the center of the glass window. It was inside the dining room. The butterfly sat on the glass pulsating its wings so beautifully. It hit me. A butterfly is one of God's earthly examples of life after death. Caterpillars crawl around struggling, trying to get somewhere (like us), then we "go to sleep" in our grave, and emerge as a beautiful butterfly which is way better than what we were before. I had always been fascinated with butterflies. How does a caterpillar become a butterfly? Big difference between the two;-one is ugly and miserable, the other beautiful and carefree.

As the months passed, it seemed like everywhere I went I would see a butterfly dart past me. If I went to the store, Zach's grave, one of my job sites, anywhere, I would see a yellow butterfly dart across my path. It didn't matter if I was driving or walking, one would always show up. It made me smile. I considered it a reminder from God of "life after death" and the joy that will come.

(More butterfly stories under "Stars")

Psalm 27:13 (niv) " *I am confident of this, I will see the goodness of the Lord in the land of the living*"

January 12, 2008

I saw two old friends today in Everglades City. They were my best friends when Zach was little. I had not seen them much in the past twenty years, just briefly here and there. They were at Zach's funeral. Their kids knew Zach through school and other various activities.

Today I saw them and they came up and gave me a big hug. They asked how I was holding up. I told them about the signs that God had been giving us regarding the birds, clouds, and the butterfly stories among others. Leigh was so amazed. She said she had never heard of anything like that. We talked a bit longer and when I turned around two beautiful brown and yellow butterflies were playing together. They looked as if they were dancing together!

March 17, 2008

Carolyn, a friend of Haven's lost her two year old daughter, Ciera. She had a seizure in her sleep and was not breathing the next morning when her mom went to get her up. Ciera was buried today. Her grave is fairly close to Zach's. Laura and Kelly, two of Haven's best friends brought fresh flowers for Zach. After the service for Ciera, we all walked over to put the flowers on Zach's grave. It was the first time the girls had been there. I went home to get a vase for the flowers. Steve went back with me. As I knelt at Zach's grave cutting and placing the flowers in the vase, Steve said, "Wow! There's a beautiful large butterfly hovering over your head." He said it was so colorful that it had to be a Monarch butterfly.

Everywhere I go, I see a yellow butterfly. I had never noticed before there were so many.

February 18, 2009

It was the day before I planned to "stop" everything and write this book. I had been doing a lot of praying about it. I've had a lot of insecurity about writing, wondering if anyone would actually be interested. I was talking to God about it, asking him to write it for me. As I was driving, I saw a cloud directly in front of me. It was shaped like a five pointed star. I laughed and told God he really does amaze me. Just as I was enjoying my amusement at God, a bird flew across the road in front of me from my left, and a yellow butterfly flew from my right. They intersected each other directly at the center of the star shaped cloud. I told Steve about it later. I thought it was so neat that God gave me a star, bird, and butterfly all at one time. Steve corrected me, he said, "He gave you a cloud, too. A bird, star, butterfly, AND cloud. Wow!"

(As you continue reading this book you will read more stories regarding clouds, stars, and birds.)

February 21, 2009

Steve and I set a date that he would go to West Virginia to visit Monica and I could stay here and write this book. Mollie, Zach's dog lives with us now, so I have to take breaks to walk her. I just finished the section on butterflies and planned to start the section on birds. I figured it was a good time to walk Mollie so I wouldn't have to stop writing during the next section.

I walked to my purse to get my sunglasses. My camera was sitting on top. I picked it up and thought, 'I should take this with me. You never know what God might have waiting for me when I go outside.' But then I second guessed myself saying I was a little bit crazy. I set the camera down and went outside.

As I walked Mollie past a neighbor's house, I reflected on how wonderful God has been and thinking about the butterfly stories I had just written. We were in front of the neighbor's driveway and a Monarch butterfly came up to us. It circled around us several times. It was so beautiful and the colors were so vibrant. I smiled at the gift I had just gotten. God you are such a mind blower. You love doing things like that for me. I love getting them too!

We went further down the road and then headed back. We got to the area the monarch butterfly had appeared earlier and along came a yellow butterfly with brown spots! It too circled around us several times and then took off to our right. I looked back to my left and just above the tree tops flying very low, a hawk flew in front of us. It circled three times above our head and then sailed off!

I guess I should have taken my camera!!

Psalms 36:5 (niv) *"Your love, O Lord, reaches to the heavens, your faithfulness to the skies"*

Romans 1:20 ((niv)/lab) *"For since the creation of the world God's invisible qualities-his external power and divine nature-have been clearly seen, being understood from what has been made, so that men are without excuse". (Nature shows us a God of might, intelligence, and intricate detail. A God of order and beauty, a God who controls powerful forces)*

## **BIRDS**

When we got back from the cruise, it was hard to come home and be reminded that Zach was gone forever. I kept telling myself to remember the signs that God had given me. I was actually holding up pretty well considering I had lost my only son. I knew it was due to the zillion prayers going up for me. I was still experiencing a roller coaster of emotions. I kept feeling guilty over everything. There were so many guilt feelings, what ifs, whys, and terrible scenarios of his last moments, along with other things that kept flooding my mind.

I picked up the coffee cup that I found in Zach's sink after he had died. I wouldn't let anyone wash it. It still had dried coffee in the bottom. I was caressing the cup and thinking about Zach drinking from it. Wondering what he had been thinking at that moment. Knowing he had no idea what was getting ready to happen. As I looked at the cup and read the poem printed on it, I noticed a picture of a bird flying as part of the background. I remembered the hand written poem we found just before the funeral and Zach's reference of watching him "fly high in the sky". I wondered what the Bible said about birds. Was there some type of relationship between the two? About that time the bird seemed to pulsate at me. It became big then small several times. Was I actually going crazy?

A day or so after this, I noticed that every time I got in my car to go somewhere or went outside, there was a single bird that looked like a hawk soaring above me. It was so graceful and majestic. It wasn't there long, but it was there *every* time. It gave me such peace and I kept remembering Zach's words *"This is your Son in the sky, Now sit back and watch me fly"*. At first I thought it was a coincidence, but then I started being aware that EVERY DAY and EVERY TIME I went out, the hawk was there. I knew the bird was a sign from God. Like God was doing this to let me know everything is going to work out for good, even though I don't understand it now. I got excited at seeing the bird each time I went out. I told everyone about it. It gave me such peace. It had even followed us when we drove to North Carolina during New Years.

A month or so had passed since Zach's death. I had not been able to go to Zach's house since the day before the funeral. Steve and I were on the way back from Ft Myers and decided to stop in and check on his house. I started crying the minute we pulled into the driveway. I got out and walked to the front door. Steve walked around to the back of the house to check the windows and stuff. I couldn't go in by myself so I stood at the front door, crying. I looked to the right to see if Steve was coming back and I saw a hawk flying in a tight circle directly above the driveway in front of our car, real low. The bird was flying even with the edge of the roof. I stood there staring at the bird as it flew in a tight circle. Then it started flying wider and higher. I thought, is this Zach? Then I said, "I love you and I miss you." It started flying higher. Two more birds joined him and they flew straight **up** out of sight. Not away, but up. It was almost like they were in the tunnel of a tornado, just not as fast.

January 12, 2008

I was outside our house talking to Chuck, a friend of Zach's. He was very discouraged and was talking about whether there really is a God. I told him about the bird and the peace it was giving me. I told him at times I was afraid to tell people about the bird because I was afraid everyone would think I was going crazy. I told him that God was so faithful in giving us signs that there really is life after death and it had been very encouraging.

Just then a bird flew across the front of my house. I pointed to the bird and said, "See, there's my bird". Just as I pointed at the bird, it made a U turn and stopped in mid air right over the area where Zach usually parked his car. Suddenly the bird WAVED its tail feathers as if to say hello and then it took off. I started laughing and looked at Chuck. I said, "Did you see that? I didn't imagine that, right?" He was smiling a huge smile and shook his head and said "Yes, that really happened."

I had NEVER seen a bird wave with its tail feathers like that before. I was so happy. I shouted out, "I love you

Zach! I love you God!" About that time another bird flew across the front of the house in the exact same path, made a U turn and stopped in the same spot, waved its tail feathers a bit longer than the bird before, and THEN the bird did a back flip and took off! I couldn't believe it! My mouth hung open in amazement. I looked over at Chuck and saw that his mouth was wide open too. We both just started laughing and I said, "*Now*, you tell me there is no God!"

February 9, 2008

Not long after the bird wave and flip, Steve and I were helping with a charity event for a friend of ours, Paul who has cancer and no insurance. A bunch of friends were putting on a Poker Run to raise some money to help with his expenses. There were approximately three hundred motorcyclists that had signed up to go place to place to collect cards for a poker hand. Each person donated money for each poker hand they would collect. Steve and I were following the motorcycles and filming the people at each location. As we were following a group of eighty bikes I told Steve that I was amazed at the kindness of people. So many people came to help us when Zach died and now look at the people helping Paul. A lot of them didn't even know him. It made me feel good. I pointed to a bird that was flying close and said, "Look at that. I'm amazed at how faithful God is to keep giving me a bird everywhere I go too." About that time the bird swooshed down towards our windshield and started flapping in front of it. It was flapping on my side just inches away as if giving us a hug or a pat on the back. We were going around 55 or 60 mph. The bird didn't touch our windshield but it was right at it. We couldn't believe it. As fast as we were going and as long as the bird stayed that close with us, I knew it was no coincidence either.

Around the same time, Haven told me she was sitting in her back yard thinking about Zach. He was supposed to come over to a party that she was going to have that night. She was sad that she would never see him again. As she sat there thinking about Zach, a large bird swooped down at her as if it were playing with her. She and Zach used to wrestle a lot when they were kids. She wondered if it was Zach still messing with her.

A couple of weeks later, Haven left our house to go home. She was still on our street when a hawk swooped down towards her windshield. It was so close that she had to stop. The bird flapped near her windshield as if it were giving her a hug and then took off. After getting over the shock of the ordeal, she started back on her way. She turned onto the main road and looked in her rear view mirror. She saw the side view of a Cadillac, like the one Zach had owned, go through her rear view mirror.

Recently my friend, Alyssa lost her husband. It was sudden and she never dreamed something like this would happen. I went to see her right away. She had never gone to church much. She had the same questions I had. Is her husband in the ground and that's it forever? Can he see her? Would God let him into Heaven?

I started sharing what I had been through and the signs God had given me. The things I had read in the Bible and the book "**Heaven**". I also warned her how the devil would give her a lot of "guilt" and "why" feelings and to not let it beat her up. I told her not to focus on herself, but to focus on what God may be trying to tell her.

I saw Alyssa at her husband's funeral. She said she had been getting a lot of signs. She was telling another friend at the funeral about my visit and signs that God gives us. She had noticed them ever since I told her they could happen. Alyssa was getting a lot of peace from them.

A few weeks later, Alyssa called me and asked if I would take her to an Easter sunrise service. I had heard of one in the Everglades with a campfire. Alyssa and her husband Mike had loved camping so I took her to that one. We were sitting outside listening to the pastor. He said, "He is Risen, He has Risen indeed" at that time for some reason Alyssa and I both turned and looked behind us. There above us was a beautiful and majestic eagle flying very low from our left. It soared directly above our heads. It was the biggest bird I had ever seen. We watched it until it flew out of site. As it disappeared,

Alyssa looked at me, smiled and said "there's another sign."

On March 10, 2008

Carolyn called Haven from Zach's grave. She was telling him to take care of Ciera. I was with Haven when Carolyn called. She told Haven not to take this the wrong way but she was glad that someone she knew was in Heaven to be with Ciera. When Haven hung up the phone she told me about the phone call. She said Carolyn was pretty upset and how she felt badly for her. I told Haven I wanted to go see Carolyn, that maybe I can help in some way.

I drove to the cemetery. When I got there, Carolyn had already left. I sat down at Zach's grave and said a prayer for Carolyn. Then I thanked God for the many signs he had given that assured me Zach was in Heaven. I asked God to help Ciera's family too. After a few minutes I got up to get some water for the flowers at Zach's headstone. When I came back, I knelt down and there was a single bird feather on Zach's grave, right at the area of Zach's heart. It had not been there earlier. I reached over and picked it up, smiling. Again, I thanked God for his faithfulness. I knew God was going to be there for this family.

April 5, 2008

Dennis, Steve and I had recently started cleaning out Zach's house. Some friends of ours had a son who was to be married soon and he and his new wife were going to rent Zach's house from us.

About a month before Zach was killed, he tiled the counter tops in his kitchen. It was hard work but he did it and was very proud. The tile stopped short of the sink. When Dennis first saw it, he told Zach that he messed it up by not putting the tile under his sink. He never told Zach what a great job he did. Everything was lined up perfectly and the cuts were symmetrical. I had thought Zach did a perfect job and was impressed with his first try at laying tile.

Dennis was feeling very guilty at how he responded to Zach's hard work. I told Dennis that Zach knows he feels bad but it's ok. He sees you looking at it and commenting on the good job he had done. He knows you didn't mean anything bad, you were just trying to teach him something. Dennis said, "Yeah, I guess you're right." I told him, "I *know* I'm right!"

Steve and I left before Dennis. A few minutes later Dennis called me all excited. He was locking Zach's front door and a hawk came down real close to his head. Then it circled around his head for a few minutes and left. He said it made him feel so good. He had heard all the previous stories about the birds and had wished he could get a sign like that. He was so excited that he had finally received his sign. He felt like Zach was telling him it really was OK.

May 23, 2008

Steve and I were painting the inside of Zach's house. I was in his bedroom crying as I painted. It was a Friday night and Memorial weekend. I imagined Zach getting ready on a Friday night and being happy that it was a long weekend. My heart was breaking in two. Steve called me to come into the kitchen real quick. I hurried to see what he wanted. Steve was standing at the sliding glass door pointing at a beautiful hawk with a baby hawk beside it. You could almost touch them. They sat on the tree limb looking at us. We smiled at the birds and they turned and flew away.

Seven months later, we were at Zach's house visiting with the couple that was renting from us. I heard a hawk cry out and asked Steve if he heard it. They told us that recently they saw a hawk sitting in the tree outside the dining room eating a snake. I smiled as I envisioned another sign that Christ has conquered the evil serpent.

My whole life I have never experienced the things I recently experienced with birds. God is in control of all creation. I KNOW He made these birds do these things to bring me peace. After all, God ordered the ravens to feed Elijah in 1 Kings 17. Why couldn't he order the birds to do flips and give hugs? All through the bible it speaks of birds and eagles being used by God. God created everything and uses everything for His glory.

1 Kings 17:4b (niv) "and I have ordered the ravens to feed you there."

I Kings 17:6 (niv) "The ravens brought him bread and meat in the morning and bread and meat in the evening,"

Revelation 8:13 (niv) *"As I watched, I heard an eagle that was flying in midair call out in a loud voice: 'Woe! Woe! Woe to the inhabitants of the earth, because of the trumpet blasts about to be sounded by the other three angels!'"*

Psalms 46:10 (niv) *"Be still and know that I am God; I will be exalted among the nations, I will be exalted in the earth"*

## **STARS**

Near the end of our cruise, Steve and I were outside on the balcony of our room. We were talking about how faithful God is to us and how blessed we are to receive so many signs after such a tragedy. I was telling him how painful it is to know I would never hug Zach again and how much I miss him. Yet I KNOW Zach is the happiest he could EVER be. The past week I had been thinking about all the things Jesus did for his disciples and believers after he rose from the grave. How he had appeared to the people on different occasions. If I believe it happened in the bible, why would I ever doubt that it could happen now? Isn't Jesus the same today as he was then? Could all these signs be similar to what Jesus did for his disciples? I started thinking about the shooting star Chris told us about and the plaque that read;

> PERHAPS THEY ARE NOT STARS IN THE SKY
> BUT RATHER OPENINGS WHERE OUR LOVED ONES SHINE DOWN
> TO LET US KNOW THEY ARE HAPPY

I started yearning to see a shooting star. Looking at my feet, I told Steve I could not remember the last time I had seen a shooting star. I looked up. Suddenly a shooting star darted across the sky! I smiled and said, "Thank you God. I really needed that."

When we got back from our trip, I received a letter from my sister, Debbie. She is Chris's mother. She wrote at the bottom of the letter that she was sitting at her table writing the letter, thinking about Zach. She sat facing her sliding glass doors as she wrote. She looked up from the letter and gazed out her sliding glass door. Darting across the sky was a shooting star. It made her smile.

After I read the letter, I called her to tell her about my star too. Then I told her about the butterfly inside the window and my revelation. She said, "Wow, do you remember what I said about the butterfly when Mollie (Zach's Dog) and I went running a few days after Zach's death?" I told her no, I hadn't heard.

She told me they walked out the door to get some exercise. A butterfly flew up to them. It stayed beside them the entire time she ran with Mollie. It didn't leave until they got back to our front door.

I asked her what color it was. She said yellow with brown spots. It was the same color as my butterfly in Antigua.

About six weeks later, Nelson, my former employer told me that he had been devastated by the news of Zach's death. He could not stop crying over it. He knew how much I adored my children, and he thought I was the best mother he had ever known. Nelson said the funeral service was the most beautiful funeral he had ever seen. He received such peace from it. He went outside of the church after the service that night. He and his wife were talking about the funeral and how peaceful it made them feel. They looked up toward heaven and saw a shooting star. Both commented as to how long it's been since they had seen one. Neither could remember *ever* seeing a shooting star before. He said he felt an even more peaceful presence after that.

December 3, 2008

My youngest sister, Maria was driving home at 1:15 am, and she was thinking about Zach and the anniversary of his death. She was praying for peace for us as we grieved. As she was praying and driving down a brightly lit road, a "super bright shooting star" shot across the sky in front of her. It was surprising to her because there are lots of lights on that road making it hard to see the sky, much less a shooting star.

Maria sent this to me by email when she got home at 2:00 am. In her letter she told me about the shooting star and that Zach said "hey" to her. "I told him how much we miss him and how much he means to us and how we can't wait to see him again."

God is amazing. He has been so faithful to give us signs all along this painful journey. It is my joy to share them with others. I hope it gives each person who reads this as much peace as it has given me.

December 13, 2008

I was at a friend's house and we were outside by the bonfire just talking to everyone. Another friend, Valerie was there with her husband, Dan. Dan's mother had died sometime in the past year or so. I was talking to the person on my right and Dan was on my left listening. I told the story about the shooting stars and how they helped me through my grief. Just as I finished saying the words, a star shot across the sky just behind the person's head. I looked at Dan and said, "Oh my gosh! Did you see that?" He said he had. Dan didn't believe in life after death.

On the way home that night Dan was thinking about what had happened. He and Valerie talked about the shooting star. When they got home, Dan got out and walked around to open the car door for Valerie. When he got up to the door, he saw two shooting stars dart across the sky. He has never seen shooting stars until that night.

I can't help but wonder if God was sending a "Hello" from Zach and Dan's mom.

January 16, 2009

Steve was walking Mollie before we went to bed for the evening. As he walked her, he thought about Zach like he always does when he walks Mollie. He was thinking about all the signs over the past year. It had been a while since he had seen any. He figured we wouldn't get any more signs now. All of the sudden, a huge star with a long tail shot in front of him. It was so close and so big that he thought it had to be fireworks or something. But he *knew* it was a star. It was unlike anything he had ever seen. It went from the east to the west just above the trees and was very close. It seemed no further away than the length of a football field.

When Steve came into the house he was all excited and sort of freaked out. He described it to me. He said it definitely was a star.

A month later, Steve called me to come in the living room right away. He had been watching the news and they reported a huge shooting star that was seen in Texas. A marathon was going on and someone had been filming the race. They caught the star on the video. The news caster played the video and said that the authorities could not find where it had landed and no one could explain what it was. It looked like a shooting star but it could not be traced. The star that they showed on the video looked exactly like the one Steve had seen a month earlier.

Ps 147:4 (niv) *"he determines the number of the stars and calls them each by name"*

Ps 19:1-2 (niv) *" The heavens declare the glory of God; the skies proclaim the work of his hands.   Day after day they pour forth speech; night after night they display their knowledge"*

## **BROKEN NECK**

Mark moonlights on weekends as a helicopter pilot for the medical flights that air lift people to the hospital. He is one of Haven's co workers. Mark was the pilot who took Zach to the hospital the night he died. He didn't know it was Haven's brother until he came to work on Monday. He and Haven were close. He loved her and treated her like a daughter. Mark told me at the funeral he was there the night of the accident. He said he would take me to the exact site of the accident if I wanted to go or if I had any questions at all to let him know. He would be glad to do anything to help us. I didn't want to impose on him through the holidays but after they were over I asked him to show us exactly where the wreck occurred.

We met at Burger King after church and he drove Dennis, Steve, and I to the location. I had so many questions that needed answers. Did Zach suffer, was he scared, did he lie there a long time before help arrived? Had the car landed on him when he was thrown out? Mark assured us that Zach did not suffer. The type of break in his neck is commonly referred to as a hangman's break. It's very quick and painless. His injuries were internal and there was very little blood. No one saw the accident happen. They used infrared scanners at the site and it was still hot, which meant it was called in fairly soon after it had happened. Zach had no pulse when the paramedics arrived. They got a pulse back and tried to airlift him to

Lee County Trauma Center. The fog was so bad they had to turn around and take him to North Collier Hospital. En route they lost his pulse again but were able to revive him. North Collier is not a trauma center and they were not equipped to handle Zach's situation. He died on the operating table. He had lost too much blood from all the internal injuries. Mark assured us that everyone did the best they could for the situation. I remembered the doctors' faces that morning. I know they felt very badly.

While we were there at the wreck site. I noticed all around us were open fields and very small trees. For three miles it was like that. There was one exception. There was a canal with a 10' wide by 3' high concrete wall in front of it. Zach's car had hit that concrete barrier and flipped several times. He was not wearing his seat belt so he was thrown from the car. If he had worn his seat belt he probably would have walked away virtually unharmed. If he had hit the small trees before or after the area, it would have slowed him down. Again, He would have walked away virtually unharmed. I was having trouble breathing again. Then I looked up and a single hawk was flying above us.

That same week, Steve was at a doctor's appointment. The doctor asked Steve about Zach's accident. Steve explained everything to him. The doctor told Steve the hangman's neck break was the same type actor Christopher Reeves had experienced. Christopher Reeves was wheel chair bound for nine years and had to have air pumped into his lungs in order to breathe. He died from pneumonia. I knew Zach would not have wanted that kind of life. He loved his freedom and being outdoors way too much to not be able to get around.

Steve's grandmother passed away the first part of February. Up until that time I cried every day. When I was around people, I tried to be tough and keep my composure. But I'd been a mess. When grandma passed away we called Steve's aunt Merla to talk about the funeral arrangements and to make sure she was doing all right. It was the first time I had talked to Merla since Zach's death. Early in the conversation, I broke down and could not talk to her. All I could do was cry and mumble how sorry I was for her loss too. She mentioned a book titled **"90 Minutes in Heaven"**. She said I needed to read it. This was on Thursday. On Sunday the author of the book was on television and Chuck, Zach's friend saw the show. He called me on Monday to tell me about the show and the book. He too said I had to read it. With all the things I've been through in my life I don't take "coincidences" lightly. I feel "coincidences" are from God and He is using these people/events as a message from Him. On Tuesday I started reading the book.

**"90 Minutes in Heaven"** is a book written by a man who died in a car accident. The man, Don Piper, was pronounced dead by several medics at the scene. Ninety minutes later while a pastor was praying over him, Don came back to life. The book describes Don's time in Heaven. His description gave me such peace. Don spent three and a half months in intensive care and another thirteen months before he was able to get out of the hospital bed. He wanted to go back to Heaven so badly. He could not understand why God would let him come back to all the pain and suffering. Since then, he has come to realize that God sent him back to help others. He has a lot of disabilities but he has been able to help people who are going through similar situations. He has offered comfort to people who have lost a loved one and encouraged others who wanted to give up. But most of all he assures people that there *really is* a Heaven. [2]

In the past year I have had three different people tell me about their "near death" experiences where they felt like they had a choice of going to heaven or staying here. They were very sure there is a moment of decision before they die or come back.

The book describes Heaven so vividly. After reading **"90 Minutes in Heaven"**, I was convinced that Zach CHOSE to stay in Heaven after dying three times. I believe that God would have allowed Zach to stay on earth, but because Heaven has no pain nor sorrow nor any of the other awful things that life offers, Zach chose to stay. If he had survived, it was very likely he would have ended up like Christopher Reeves. I know he didn't want that kind of life.

A woman I've known casually for fifteen years had lost her son around the time I first met her. He was dead when she went to wake him up one morning. She was very torn up about it and I figured it must have been due to a drug overdose or something. He was twenty five years old. Not really knowing her at the time, I didn't ask any questions. Not long after I had read "**90 Minutes in Heaven**" I was talking to the lady on the phone. She asked me how I had been that she had not talked to me in a while. I told her about Zach and she started crying. She had not heard the news. Three days later she called me and said she wanted to tell me about her son who had died fifteen years earlier. Her son had a wreck when he was nineteen years old and suffered a hangman's break. He had lived for six years after the accident. She told some of the struggles they had faced physically and emotionally in the years following his accident. It made me realize that God had blessed us by letting Zach die right away instead of letting him suffer. We could have spent years watching Zach struggle to live a somewhat normal life. We would be wishing and hoping for the best for him and still end up with the same result, death.

It had been almost a year since Zach's accident and I was crying a lot lately. I kept reliving the day of the accident. I was trying to work and keep my mind busy. I had stopped by one of my suppliers where a woman who worked there started telling me about her son moving away and how she was upset over it. I told her about my mother crying when I moved from North Carolina to Florida. Mom had told God she was upset over my move. He said clearly to her, "Be Glad that it's distance, not death that separates you." When I said that to her, she remembered that my son had died. She said she was sorry and that she was being selfish. I told her I totally understood. Mothers love their children more than anything on this earth.

She told me about her husband who was disabled from a broken neck. They had been married a few years and had two little children when it happened. They were on a family vacation and her husband dove into a lake and broke his neck. He had been paralyzed for almost thirty years. She was telling me about the struggles of going to restaurants and other public places. It was so difficult that he rarely left the house. Because of that, he was very bitter and angry. He refused to wear any type of diaper and would urinate and defecate in his chair or all over the floor. She would come home after a hard day of work and have to clean the mess. She said it hurt her so much to see him like that. They both were always angry and upset as they struggled with his situation. Tears started streaming down her face as she said, "I think it would have been better if he had just died when he dove into the lake. At least he would have been a lot happier." I went to her and hugged her and we held each other and cried. Her husband and my son both suffered a broken neck. She cried because her husband lived, I cried because my son had died.

God's plan is so much bigger than anything we can imagine.

## **CLOUDS**

Four weeks had passed by since Zach's death. It was the week between Christmas and New Years and Steve and I decided to take a quick trip to North Carolina where most of my family lives. My mother was having a hard time dealing with Zach's death, plus she kept worrying about me. (You know how it is, as a parent, it hurts so badly when your children are hurting and you can't do anything about it.) I thought it would be good to show them I really was doing all right. Naturally I had been on a roller coaster of emotions but I kept reminding myself all this is for a reason. I *will* TRUST GOD.

On the drive to NC, Steve and I talked constantly for ten hours. It was really the first time we actually had a conversation with my being somewhat coherent and without any distractions. My cell phone was off, the radio was off, just Steve and I talking. Early in our trip I was telling Steve that it's weird when something horrible happens to you, how doubts and questions keep popping into your mind. I had actually wondered if Heaven was real or if we just stayed in the ground and that was it. I told him that the thought occurred several times but only lasted a second because in my heart I REALLY KNOW that Heaven IS real. I was so thankful that God had been so good to me to show me very clearly that He is real and so is His promise of Heaven. As I finished saying this to Steve, I looked out the side window of the car up at the sky. Right there all by itself was a big fluffy white cloud with a hole cut all the way thru to the blue sky. The hole was shaped like a perfect heart! I couldn't believe it. I told Steve to look but one side of the cloud moved over and closed up the opening so he didn't see it. I realized it was a special post card just for me from Heaven. God was telling me that my heart was in the right place and He loved me.

A few days later, Haven was outside her house and was thinking about Zach. She looked up to the sky. She saw an "H" and an "I" in the clouds. She ran to get her camera and told her boyfriend to come look. They both looked at it. She tried to take a picture but it would not show up in the camera. But without question, they both saw the perfect shape of the word "HI" made out of clouds.

There were several times that things had happened to Haven and me where we tried to take a picture of it, but for some reason it would not show up in the camera. We knew we had not imagined the things we saw as we usually had a witness. We could only attribute it to a "God Thing".

Another friend Paula lost their husband Bill due to a heart attack. She never dreamed something like this could happen. Haven and I went to see her right away. Their family didn't go to church. They were always busy with sports or work. She was worried about where her husband's soul had gone.

Haven and I shared with her what we had been through and the signs God had given us. I asked her if Bill believed in God and she said yes. When he was a young boy his parents took him to church. I told her about Zach's tattoo and how God does not take away our salvation once we accepted it. I told her that the devil is the author of death and God was the giver of life. People confuse this fact when faced with the death of a loved one. They immediately blame God.

Her twenty four year old daughter, Jessica was very angry at God for letting this happen. I warned Paula how the devil would give them a lot of "guilt" and "why" feelings and to not let it eat them up. A few days later at the funeral, Jessica came up to me and thanked me for talking to her mom. Paula had shared with her children what I had told her. They all felt so much better than they did at first. I gave Jessica a small booklet that is a cliff note version of the book, **Heaven** by Randy Alcorn. I told her this would help answer a lot of her questions and I would be there for them any time they ever needed to talk.

On the way home from Bill's funeral service, Easter Sunday night, Steve and I were talking about how well Paula and her daughter and the rest of the family were doing. There was a noticeable difference from a few days earlier when they were all mad at God. Steve was driving and excitedly said "Look" and pointed to the sky. There in front of us was a cloud that looked perfectly like the sign language sign for "I Love You". It was very distinct. You could see the shape of each finger. Steve put his hand up to the windshield to match it up and it fit perfectly. I put mine up and it too fit perfectly. I said, "Oh my gosh! God is telling us that he is proud of us and He loves us!!"

Our family gave the "I love you" sign every time we drove away from each other. It started when Zach would not let me kiss him in front of the school when I dropped him off each morning. We had used this sign for over sixteen years.

As clouds usually do, the winds started shifting the clouds. As the "I love you" sign shifted, it changed into the shape of an eagle with its wings spread and head turned, similar to what you see on currency. It reminded me of the words you see around the eagle….."In God We Trust".

All this happened on Easter Sunday, Alyssa's eagle earlier that morning and our "I love you" cloud. The same day I had read the story that Jesus tells in Luke 16 of a Rich man and Lazarus where they see each other after death. Lazarus had been a beggar who would lie at the rich man's gate in hope of getting his table scraps. They both died. The rich man went to Hell and Lazarus was taken by the angels to be with Abraham in Heaven. The rich man looked up and saw Abraham far away with Lazarus by his side. They were separated by a great chasm but could talk to each other. The rich man begged Lazarus to dip his finger in water to cool his tongue. Abraham tells him that the chasm was fixed and no one could go from one side to the other. The rich man begged Abraham to send Lazarus to his father's house to tell his family that Hell is real. But Abraham said no. He explained that they have what Moses and the Prophets left for them telling of this place. If they did not listen to the Prophets, they would not be convinced if someone rises from the dead and comes to them. (Luke 16:19-31) Sound familiar? Jesus rose from the dead and today a lot of people don't believe it.

April 5, 2008

Dennis and Steve were at Zach's house cleaning out the bottom of his stilt house. I had been taking a lot of stuff to his house so we could finish off the lower level and make it into living area. Now that Zach was gone, we didn't want to do it. We decided to throw the stuff away. Most of it had come from houses we had remodeled. I was going to a surprise birthday party for a friend of mine. As I was driving to the party I was thinking about the guys cleaning up the bottom. Suddenly I saw a distinct "smiley face" in the clouds. I wondered if Zach was laughing at Dennis and Steve for cleaning under his house and was glad that he didn't have to help!

April 7, 2008

Today Steve called our friend Paul, who has cancer. Paul was happy to hear from Steve. No one had been to visit him and he was pretty depressed. When Steve hung up, he started to pray for Paul. He worried that he might not make it through the cancer. As he prayed Steve started thinking about Zach and said, "I can't believe he died. It's just so hard to believe." As Steve turned onto the street leading to one of our customer's house, he looked up and directly in front of him was a perfect cross cut out in the middle of a bunch of clouds. He realized that Zach wasn't dead, but that he was alive in Heaven. Thanks to Jesus who died on the cross. God used the clouds to remind Steve of this.

May 23, 2008

My heart was breaking in two. It was the hardest day that I'd had in Zach's house since he left. I could see Zach's smile and remembered the way he made people laugh. Everyone said he was the coolest and funniest person they had ever met.

On the way home I was still thinking about Zach. I turned off the interstate and headed east on Immokalee Rd. Directly in front of me was a sky full of white fluffy clouds. In front of the white clouds was one very dark cloud shaped like a heart but with a tail like a kite. It was huge. It looked like somebody was telling me they loved me even in my darkness. Hmmmm....

July 23, 2008

I was talking to one of our customers today and she started asking if I have any children. I told her yes, I have three. She asked what they did and where they lived. I spoke about both daughters and tried to avoid the part about Zach. But she kept pushing for info on my son. I finally said he lives in Heaven. Her face dropped and she asked what happened. I explained briefly. Then I told her God had been very faithful in letting me know for sure that Zach *truly* lives in heaven. I shared some of the events with her. As I spoke, an eagle appeared behind her so I pointed it out. (Even now I still have a bird show up every day at my every location.) She then told me about her son who has a genetic disease that made it very likely he would not live past the age of forty two. He had just turned forty two. Her husband's brother, father, and other male relatives all died with this disease. Her biggest fear was losing her son. I told her I could relate to *that* feeling. She said he had almost died several times over the years, just going through that was almost too much for her to bear. I assured her that heaven was real and her son would go there as long as he believed in God. I told her not to be afraid and that he is in good hands with God. He actually loves her son more than she does.

The next day I was driving home and the traffic stopped for a light. I was stopped even with Zach's wreck site. I looked at it and starting hyperventilating. I had such an ache inside that I was not sure I could take the next breath. I started crying and talking to God. I remembered the eagle from yesterday and all the other unbelievable signs. I thanked God for all of them and His faithfulness to me. I told Him how amazed I was at His love and asked him to forgive me when I hurt so much. I told God that I missed Zach and to please give him a big hug from me.

The cemetery was not far from the wreck site. I pass by both almost every day. I turned to look towards the traffic light. Beyond the light, the clouds were shaped like an arm and hand stretched out with a pointed finger. At the end of the pointed finger was a backwards "Z". It was in the direction of the cemetery and my eyes could not believe what I saw. I grabbed my camera and took a picture. By this time there was a backwards Z, a little puff ball and then a "c" all going right to left. It was completely backwards.

The light turned green and traffic started moving. As I got closer to the cemetery the little puff ball turned into a little "a". I was looking at "Zac" spelled backwards as if looking at a mirror. The clouds were dark all over the sky except for the opening showing the arm and the letters. The "c" was at the edge of the opening. I guessed there was probably an "h" just past the opening. Thankfully the picture turned out this time. I knew no one would *ever* believe this one!

Just a few weeks before this happened, I was at church. Jim our friend was preaching from the book of Daniel. He told the story of Belshazzar and the hand that appeared out of the sky writing a warning from God. Jim paused as he told of the hand and said, "Pretty amazing, huh? I think it would be mighty scary to see something like that." I remember thinking, 'yeah it would definitely freak me out, but if it's in the Bible, I believe it happened.' It's only been a couple of weeks since that sermon. Wow God!

Psalms 77:11 (niv) *"I will remember the deeds of the Lord; yes, I will remember your miracles of long ago"*

Hebrews 13:8 (niv) *"Jesus Christ is the same yesterday and today and forever."*

September 20, 2008

Haven's friend Kelly lost her brother, Denny this week to a freak ATV accident. Denny and his parents had moved to north Florida approximately eighteen months ago. Kelly and her sister, Lindsey still live in Naples. The funeral was being held today. We did not go to north Florida as the family was planning on having a memorial service here too.

Steve and I had been in constant prayer for the family. We understood the pain they were experiencing. When Zach had died, Denny's mom was so heartbroken for us. She mentioned many times that she could not imagine going through the loss of a child. I felt so badly that she was now experiencing this same unbearable pain.

Steve was driving to a job and passed the cemetery where Zach was buried. He thanked God for all the things he had done for us and asked him to please do the same for Denny's family. He asked God to give them peace and comfort. As he prayed for them, he stopped at a light. Slightly to the left there was a cloud formation all by itself with no other clouds. The formation was a "Z" and a "C" touching with an outline of a heart shape at the center where the two letters touched. Steve took a picture of the cloud. It was so beautiful. He knew God had heard his prayer.

Jeremiah 10:13b (niv) *"he makes clouds rise up from the ends of the earth"*

Psalms 147:8 (niv) *"He covers the sky with clouds"*

## **EASTER**

In the movie *The Passion of Christ* there is a scene where the rulers sneered at Jesus when he was on the cross. They said "He saved others; let him save himself if he is the Christ of God, the Chosen One." One of the criminals beside Jesus said "Aren't you the Christ? Save yourself and us!" The other criminal rebuked him telling him "Don't you fear God, since we are under the same sentence? We are punished justly, for we are getting what our deeds deserve. But this man has done nothing wrong". He then asked Jesus to remember him when he comes into his kingdom. Jesus answers the criminal, "I tell you the truth, today you will be with me in paradise." (Luke 23:35-43)

Watching that scene it dawned on me that unbelievers say "SHOW ME A MIRACLE AND I WILL BELIEVE" but GOD SAYS "BELIEVE, AND I WILL SHOW YOU MIRACLES"

I *do* believe in God. I am human and have my ups and downs but I always try to Trust God. I know that He has my best interest in mind. Even when I felt betrayed and forgotten by God, He remained faithful in His love for me.

Zach is in Heaven with Jesus. My son is the happiest he could ever imagine. He has no more past due bills, no more toothaches, no more worries, no one taking advantage of him. He's wrestling with alligators, surfing on the backs of whales, jumping off waterfalls, and probably jumping from tree to tree exploring the Intermediate Heaven where Christians go when they die. I miss my son terribly, but I know he is with God and together they are speaking very loudly to me and my family. I look forward to the day when I can see my son again. When that happens, it will be total joy forever and nothing will ever separate us again.

## **THE RADIO**

On the drive to North Carolina during the New Year's holiday, Steve and I had talked for over ten hours.

Around 9:00 that night we were still driving but had tired of talking so I turned on the radio. I searched the stations until I found a song I liked. When the song ended, the DJ started talking about a story they had aired last year. It was about a famous sports figure that had lost his nineteen year old son just before Christmas in 2005. They had many requests to air it again as it had made such an impact on so many lives. It was a speech the father had given at a Super bowl breakfast two months after the death of his son. The speaker was Tony Dungy. I remembered hearing about his son's death and how everyone was making a big deal about Tony returning to work so soon afterwards. I turned up the volume.

Tony Dungy spoke at his son's funeral. He said his biggest regret is that he didn't give his son, James a hug the last time he saw him during Thanksgiving. His son left for the airport and all they said to each other was "See you later".

The day after James' funeral a man who had attended the funeral took off work to spend the day with his son. They went to the movies, had dinner, and enjoyed various things throughout the day. Tony's regrets made this man realize he would have quite a few of his own if his son were to die. The man called Tony and said that his speech at the funeral had been a real blessing to him. James death had brought this man and his son closer and he vowed to pay more attention to his own son.

The Dungy family donated James' corneas and helped two people to see again. A young girl who had sat by James in church her whole life never really knew if there was a God or not. She told Tony after seeing his family and the celebration at the funeral that she now knew there was a God and had asked Christ into her heart that day.

Another young man called Tony and told him he had thought about taking his own life but he changed his mind after he attended James' funeral.

A close friend of the Dungy family who knew about the changes in these people said to Tony, "If God had said to you, 'I can help people see, heal relationships, save lives, and give someone eternal life, **IF** you give up your son's life.' Would you give him up?" The friend reminded Tony that God did it for us two thousand years ago with his son Jesus Christ. He then asked, "James accepted Christ into his heart so you know he's in heaven, right?" Tony said, "Yes". The friend continued… "Well, with all you know about Heaven and if you had the power to bring James back, would you?"[3]

I knew the answer to both of the questions regarding Zach. No, I wouldn't give him up and No, I wouldn't try to bring him back.

Steve and I were amazed this story had aired right then. Was God talking to us? The timing and the message could not have been better scripted! Steve pointed out that similar things had happened since Zach's death. Many people in the past month had told us that Zach's funeral changed them. One person said that if anyone in that room wasn't a believer before, they sure were now. A friend said she looked at her children so differently now. That putting up the Christmas tree with her kids this year was different. She vowed to become a better parent and spend more time with her kids.

I had given the Police Officer that worked Zach's case a copy of Zach's poem and had shared a lot of things with him regarding God's faithfulness to us. He later told me that he kept Zach's letter on his bulletin board at work. He said it gave him hope. (We've talked several times since Zach's death. I know that this wreck has changed the Officer's life.)

A lady that is a Buddhist was touched by the Poem left by Zach and the things that were said at Zach's funeral. She said, "God is very present in these people's life." It was the first time ever the woman had acknowledged God.

There were a lot of people at Zach's funeral. At least half of the people there were not Christians. I know Zach's death will help save souls. I'm beginning to understand now. *Romans 8:32 (niv) "He who did not spare his own Son, but gave him up for us all-how will he not also, along with him, graciously give us all things?"*

The prayers must have slacked off right after Christmas and our trip to North Carolina. Even though I was sure of God's love, there was something that still wasn't right with me. I started crying more and more. I wasn't able to function very well. I felt like I was going through the motion of living but not really there. One day I was crying so hard and I had a million things to do but I just could not stop crying. Steve left the house and tried to take care of some of the things but he was very worried about me. He called a few times but I couldn't talk. All I could do was cry. My mornings and nights were the worst. It was late morning and I had been crying for four hours. I finally told myself I had to get a grip and get on with living. I got in my car and started it. The first thing I heard from the radio was "God cares for you and wants to heal your hurts; He loves you and wants you to talk to him." I stared at the radio. I listened to the message some more. It was everything I needed to hear at that moment. God keeps using everything around me to talk to me. A peace came over me.

I called Steve to tell him what happened and I would be all right. Steve said, "I'm at the cemetery with Zach right now. I was just thanking him and God for the signs they had been giving you letting you know he was alright, and asking him to continue giving you signs. Then the phone rang. It was you calling to tell me about the message on the radio."


Psalms 27:13 (niv) *"I am still confident of this; I will see the goodness of the Lord in the land of the living"*

**ONLY SON**

October 26, 2008
It was Zach's birthday. He would have been twenty six years old today. I woke up crying. I remembered the day he was born and all the joy he had brought to me in the twenty five years he was here. He was so kind and compassionate, so full of honor. He was an extremely handsome young man. He told me once that he hoped to be married and start a family by the time he was twenty five.

I told Steve I needed to go to Zach's grave by myself and talk to God a bit. I took a blanket, a box of Kleenex, Zach's picture, and a birthday balloon. It was very early in the morning and no one was around. I sat there just bawling for over an hour and a half. I remembered his last birthday with us and all the other ones before it.

Birthdays were a big deal at my house. I always celebrated God's gift of "you" with each one of my kids. I would decorate their rooms while they were sleeping so they could feel happy when they woke up. I had not done the decorating for Zach since he moved into his own home but I still made a big deal out of birthdays.

The ache I was experiencing at this moment was unbearable. After crying and reliving memories for over an hour, I talked to God about my hurt. I asked him to help me get through this time. Suddenly a peace came over me. I knew God heard my prayer. I felt such calm all the way through my entire being.

I looked at Zach's headstone. The date of his heavenly birth illuminated at me. It was almost as if it was pulsing. The number **12 1 7** kept pulsing like a heartbeat.  A thought popped into my head, **twelve** disciples, **one** Savior, **seven** years. I got chills all over. I wondered if God had taken Zach to heaven to prepare him to fight in God's army for when the end times come. I know it sounds weird but it was so real and the thought was so clear!

The number **twelve** and the number **seven** have a lot of meaning in the Bible. Throughout the entire Bible these numbers hold great significance. I told Steve what happened when I got home. He was surprised at how peaceful I seemed compared to when I left earlier. I wasn't sure if I should tell anybody else what had happened.  They may decide to call the paddy wagon!

The number thing happened to me on Sunday.  On Tuesday I told Haven about the warrior thought and the pulsating numbers. She just looked at me and didn't say much about it. (She was probably thinking about calling that paddy wagon!)  Friday of the same week Haven told me that she had been at her friend Kelly and Lindsey's the night before. (Their brother, Denny was killed last month in an ATV accident.)

Their dad was in church this past Sunday. His heart was aching so badly. He was sitting there thinking, begging, "God, *why* did you take my only son?" Suddenly he heard a very loud and distinct voice say, "Look over there," (it was a large statue of Jesus hanging on the cross) "that's my son and he died too. But your son didn't experience any pain, mine did. I know it is hard to understand, but I needed your son for a reason."

Haven said it gave her chills when Kelly told her this. She thought about what had happened to me on that same Sunday. She wondered if Denny was a warrior too.

The next week I went back to Zach's grave. I had been thinking about the numbers all week. I knelt down to pray. As I looked at the headstone I realized the months were abbreviated, not numerical form as I had seen them last. Instead of **12 1 7**, I saw Dec 1 2007. Chills ran through my body.

I thought about all the people we knew that have died in the past year. There were seventeen of them. Two thirds were male and many had served in the military.

I wonder what's next….

Isaiah 54:13 (niv) *"All your sons will be taught by the Lord, and great will be your children's peace."*

Luke 15:21,24 (niv)  vs21 *"The son said to him, 'Father, I have sinned against heaven and against you. I am not* worthy to be your son.' Vs24 " 'For this son of mine was dead and is alive again; he was lost and is found.' So they began to celebrate"

Exodus 34:19 (niv) *"the first offspring of every womb belongs to me, including all the first born males of your livestock,…"*

Romans 8:28 (niv) *"and we know that in all things God works for the good of those who love him, who have been called according to his purpose.*

1 Samuel 1:28 (niv) *"Now I am giving him to the Lord, and he will belong to the Lord his whole life."*

John 13:7 (niv) **"Jesus replied, 'you do not realize now what I am doing, but later you will understand.'"**

## **IDOLS**

Early after Zach's death, our church had a sermon about Idols. It occurred to me that I had actually turned my son into an idol. I realized when I was at his grave I would pray to Zach. Steve had been doing it too. I told Steve what we were doing and he agreed. We went to Zach's grave and asked God to forgive us. We knew it was ok to talk *to* Zach, but it wasn't ok to ask him to give us signs or other things to give us peace. This could only be done through God. God controls the universe, not Zach. I felt so ashamed when I realized what I had been doing. Thankfully God forgave us. Now we make sure we are praying to the right person when we go there.


## **PSYCHICS:**

Two of our friends contacted "Mediums" after their loved ones passed away. I wanted to tell them that this is totally wrong but I was having a hard time telling them. I tried but they were so excited at what the "medium" told them. It actually scared me.

God is very, **very** specific in His word about this.

In Daniel 2, Nebuchadnezzar was troubled over a dream. He sought magicians, sorcerers and astrologers to tell him what he had dreamed. Today, we have a tendency to turn to other "things" when we are troubled. This includes things such as friends, drugs, alcohol, violence etc. as well as mediums or psychics.   The real answer is to PRAY and TRUST God.  God chooses who can interpret dreams, not us.

Leviticus 19:31(MSG) *"don't dabble in the occult or traffic with mediums; you'll pollute your souls.  I am God, your God."*

Leviticus 20:6 (MSG)  *"I will resolutely reject persons who dabble in the occult or traffic with mediums, prostituting themselves in their practices.  I will cut them off from their people."* [4]

"God warned about looking to the occult for advice.  Mediums and Spiritists were outlawed because God was not the source of their information.  At best, occult practitioners are fakes whose predictions cannot be trusted.  At worst, they are in contact with evil spirits and are thus extremely dangerous.  We don't need to look to the occult for information about the future.  God has given us the Bible so that we may obtain all the information we need-and the Bible's teaching is trustworthy."[5]

1 Samuel 28:9 (MSG)  *"The woman said, 'just hold on now!  You know what Saul did, how he swept the country clean of mediums.  Why are you trying to trap me and get me killed?'"*

"Practioners of the occult have Satan and demons as the source of their information; God does not reveal his will to them, instead he speaks through his own channels: the Bible, his Son Jesus Christ, and the Holy Spirit." [6]

Don't pray to your lost loved one. Don't Focus on getting in touch with the deceased, instead focus more on God's purpose for taking them.

When the woman drummed up Samuel's spirit from the ground she screamed. (1 Samuel 28:12 paraphrased) Why would she scream if she believed it would happen? This is a sign that she normally did not see a **real** spirit.

Stormie Omartian describes it very well in her book THE POWER OF PRAYING on pg 68-"Sometimes we are caught in the midst of the enemy's work. It's the enemy's delight to make you miserable and try to destroy your life. Often the reason for the anguish, sorrow, sadness, grief, or pain you feel is entirely his doing and no fault of your own or anyone else's. Your comfort is in knowing that as you praise God in the midst of it, He will defeat the enemy and bring good out of it that you can't even fathom. He wants you to walk with Him in faith as He leads you through it, and He will teach you to trust Him in the midst of it."[7]

Jeremiah 2:5b (niv) *"they followed worthless idols and became worthless themselves."*

Psalm 118:17-18 (niv) *"I will not die but live, and will proclaim what the Lord has done. The Lord has chastened me severely, but he has not given me over to death."*

## **DREAMS**

Aysha, Zach's first cousin had a dream about him one night. It was about five weeks after his death. She dreamed that she was at the airport. Zach was sitting in the driver's seat of a car waiting for her. He asked her where she was going. She told him she was going to his funeral. He told her it wasn't necessary, that he was all right. She said it was so real.

April 3, 2008

Monica called from West Virginia all excited. She'd had a dream about Zach the night before. She said that Zach was able to come back to earth for one day and we were all sitting at our dining room table laughing and eating. Everyone was so happy in her dream. She said it was so real and such a wonderful and peaceful feeling. There was such happiness all around. She said Zach had the biggest smile she had ever seen on him. She remembers being able to touch him, it was so real.

As the kids were growing up, we made sure that our family had meals together. When they all grew up and moved away, it was one of the things each one said they missed the most. So do I. (God promises meals and fellowship when we get to Heaven. I'll bet that will be some really good eating!!)

Also around this time, Monica had another dream about her grandmother, Steve's mom, who had died seven years earlier from breast cancer. It was the first time Monica had dreamed of her grandmother since she had passed away. In the dream Monica saw her and asked if she knew that Zach had died. She answered, "Yes, I know. He's here with me".

April 19, 2008

I went to bed missing Zach so badly. I wished that I could hug him. I had been telling God how much I missed Zach's hugs. During the night, I had a dream about Zach. I told him I needed a hug. That was all I remember of the dream.

When I woke up the next morning, I felt like I'd had the biggest hug of my life. The entire front part of the trunk of my body was soooooo warm. My arms, legs, and back were normal, just my front felt warm. I just know the Holy Spirit was there hugging me. I couldn't think of any other reason why the front my body would be so warm and the rest of me cool and normal.

April 23, 2008

I went to bed thinking about Zach's gun accident. It was three years ago last night when the accident happened.

During the night I woke up and saw something red similar to cracked glass covering my bathroom door. At first I thought it was our pool reflecting on the door. I laid back down and started thinking how odd this red glass looked.

I sat back up and looked at the door again. The "vision" was a full size head with thorns around it, like Jesus wore. The vision was within the red cracked glass. It disappeared and to the right of it stood two men talking. This too disappeared and to the right was Jesus kneeling beside a child with his hand on the child's head. Again, the vision disappeared and the next vision was Jesus sitting down holding a baby. It was if I had been watching a slide show. Each "person" looked similar to Zach at each age that was shown. The other person was Jesus as he wore the crown of thorns in each "vision". I wondered what it meant. Was it Zach's life in reverse?

Was this "vision" telling me that *Jesus died for our sins, he talked with Zach, laid his hands on Zach's head to forgive him, everything was removed, and all was forgotten. The baby was a sign that all was clean and pure again*?

A New Beginning?

Romans 5:1 (niv) *"Therefore since we have been justified through faith we have peace with God through our Lord Jesus Christ, through whom we have gained access by faith into this grace in which we now stand, and rejoice in the hope of the glory of God."*

Philippians 3:20 (niv) *"But our citizenship is in heaven. And we eagerly await a Savior from there, the Lord Jesus Christ, who by the power that enables him to bring everything under his control will transform our lowly bodies so that they will be like his glorious body."*

Mark 10:16 (niv) *"and he took the children in his arms, put his hands on them and blessed them"*

May 6, 2008

Last night I had a snap shot dream about Zach. I dreamed he was walking from my house towards the driveway. He then turned around and was smiling a HUGE BEAUTIFUL smile. He had his right arm extended towards me with his hand opened. It was like he was saying, "Come with me." It was a short dream but very clear. He was *extremely* happy.

The snap shot dream that I had last night reminded me of something that I had noticed the night Zach was in the hospital. It didn't really register until now.

When we went into the room after they told us he didn't make it, I started touching Zach's face and arm. I was trying to be strong but the tears were streaming down my face so hard. I prayed over him and lovingly touched every inch of his face then went down his arm until I came to his hand. I remember taking his hand and it had fit perfectly into my own. It was almost like a hand had been there and my hand had slipped into its place. Steve mentioned later that he shook Zach's hand that night and it had fit perfectly into his.

In the book "**90 MINUTES IN HEAVEN**", Don Piper mentioned someone had held his right hand while he was trapped in the car. He found out later that it was totally impossible for anyone to get to his right hand as it had been trapped within the wreckage below the glove compartment.

I'm not sure if it was Jesus or an angel, but someone was there holding Zach's hand the night he died. Maybe my dream last night was a small insight of that.

Psalm 138:7 (niv) *"you reach out your hand, and the power of your right hand saves me."*


May 9, 2008

I found a letter that I had written to Zach soon after his gun accident. I had never given it to him for some reason. I read it and cried so hard. Why hadn't I sent it to him? It could have helped him so much. There were several scripture verses listed throughout the letter. It was just the book, chapter, and verse. I had not written the words to each one. There was one in particular that had a larger font. I decided to look it up. It was Psalm 116:1-9 (niv). Verse 3 stuck with me, *"The cords of death entangled me, the anguish of the grave came upon* me; I was overcome by trouble and sorrow."  There was a reference beside this verse to 2 Samuel 22:6.  I decided to look it up.  For some reason I stopped at verses 17-20.  When I read it, I felt like God was talking to me again.

I decided to go back to the original chapter in Psalms 116 but I stopped at Psalm 18:16-19.  It just jumped at me.  I could not believe it.  It was word for word what I had just read in 2 Samuel.  I've read the Bible a lot in my life but never have I read two verses word for word in two different chapters.  There may be others, but this was my first time.  Here are the verses:

2 Samuel 22:17-20  (niv)  /  Psalm 18:16-19  (niv)

***"He reached down from on high and took hold of me; he drew me out of deep waters.  He rescued me from my powerful enemy, from my foes, who were too strong for me.  They comforted me in the day of my disaster, but the Lord was my support.  He brought me out into a spacious place; he rescued me because he delighted in me."***


"Do your troubles, like "deep waters," threaten to drown you? David, helpless and weak, knew that God alone had rescued him from his enemies when he was defenseless.  When you wish that God would quickly rescue you from your troubles, remember that he can either deliver you or be your support as you go through them.  Either way, his protection is best for you.  When you feel like you're drowning in troubles, ask God to help you, hold you steady, and protect you.  In his care, you are never helpless."[8]

110

## **CARDS/BOOKS**

February 26, 2008

My dad's best friend lost his son about six weeks ago. I felt I should write them a letter of encouragement as I understood what they were going through. I sat down to write the letter and prayed for the right words. My fingers just ran across the computer keys and I was actually surprised at the letter. I knew it was God inspired. I keep a box of cards for different occasions. When I see something I like in the store, I buy it and put it in the box. I decided to look in the box for a sympathy card to send with the letter. I opened the first sympathy card I found and to my utter amazement, there in Zach's hand writing were the words, "Keep Praying, Love Zach" I must have given it to him to sign sometime in the past to send to someone else. Little did I know that he was signing it for me to read after his own death.

March 22, 2008

Birthdays have always been a big deal at our house. My birthday is in November, but we didn't celebrate it last year because Zach had a really bad toothache and didn't feel like getting together. Less than a month later he died. I kept feeling depressed that I didn't have a card from Zach to read on my future birthdays. The thought kept entering my head and I kept telling myself I was being silly. I didn't need a card to remember Zach.

I was looking through some old papers and I ran across an envelope that had "MOM" written on it. It was in Zach's hand writing. It looked like it had never been opened. (It had one of those gold stickers on the back to seal it closed.) I started shaking as I opened the envelope. It *was* a birthday card from Zach. It was so beautiful. The front of the card read:

**For My Mom**

**A Loving Birthday Wish From Your Son**

Inside it read:

I know I don't have to wait until your birthday
to let you know how much I appreciate you.
But you know how I am—
I've always had a hard time
putting my feelings into words.
I guess I just assume they're understood.
Anyway, what I'm trying to say
is that I love you, Mom, not just on your birthday
but always.

Happy Birthday
Love,
Zach


I guess I got my birthday card after all.

Zach wrote the poem that we found just before his funeral on June 15, 2007. His friend's sister owns a book called "The Brotherhood of Life". She said it is a book that tells the significance of certain dates. She looked up the date of June 15. The book said this date means "PERFECT BALANCE BETWEEN HEAVEN and EARTH". I must say God was definitely guiding Zach that night for future events.

There is a man I met at the cemetery. His name is Al and he is eighty four years old. His wife died in October. Every day Al would sit at his wife's grave for hours. He had not missed a day since she passed away. He doesn't believe in Heaven and wonders what his wife is going through in death. Dennis, Steve, and I have tried to help Al but he just refuses to let us take him to dinner or do anything but sit at his wife's graveside.

One day Dennis said I should give Al the books I had given him which had helped Dennis a lot. A few days later, I gave Al the book **"90 Minutes in Heaven"**. I had marked the pages where Don Piper described his trip to heaven. Then I gave Al a sixty page booklet that was a simplified version of the book **"Heaven"** by Randy Alcorn. I marked things in red that I thought would help him.

Every Sunday Dennis goes to Zach's grave. Al always saw him there but never left his wife's grave to talk to him. Dennis and Steve and I would go visit Al by his area. The Sunday after I gave Al the books he came running across the cemetery to see Dennis. He was very excited. He was like a little kid. Al said the books were awesome and thanked Dennis over and over for telling him about them. He really appreciated my giving them to him. Dennis said Al was running excitedly all over the cemetery telling everyone about the books. Everyone was smiling at him. Al was finally getting a glimpse that Heaven is real.

Al and I are good friends to this day. He finally went out to dinner with Steve and me. We've enjoyed many meals together since then.

People who come into our lives are there for a reason. We should pay more attention to them instead of just passing by them as if they were invisible.

Once I had read the book **"Heaven"** and discovered the sixty page booklet, I've bought cases of them and given them out. Dennis told me a story about the **"Heaven"** booklet I had given him a few months earlier. He had never read it. It was tucked in the middle of a bunch of books on his end table.

One night Dennis was lying on his couch in the living room grieving over the loss of Zach. He fell asleep sometime later. When he woke up the **"Heaven"** booklet was on the arm of the couch just above his head. He had no idea how it got there. The lights were not on and there was no one else in the house. He wondered if it was some type of sign.

MOTHER'S DAY

My children made me feel special all the time. On Mother's day they really went out of their way to love on me. Every year since they were very little, they made me breakfast in bed. As the years went by, Zach got better at cooking which was something he loved doing. I looked forward to eating his masterpiece each year.

After Zach moved into his own home, he still made a point of making me feel special on Mother's day. He would do things like ask me to meet him for dinner at a restaurant. He would stand outside waiting for me with a single yellow rose. He would walk to the car door, open it, and then help me out. He was such a true gentleman. I knew he would be a wonderful husband some day.

This Mother's Day I was obviously depressed. I remembered past Mother's Days spent with my son. My heart was breaking thinking there would be no more. I was still fighting off the devil as he was constantly throwing negative thoughts into my head. This holiday I was beating myself up wondering if Zach knew how much the things he had done for me in years past had meant to me. I felt I had taken them for granted.

Father's day came and again I relived past Mother's days. I was aching so much inside. I really missed my son. One day soon after, I was cleaning up some papers that were piled up in my daughter's old room. I had been cramming stuff in there after she moved out just to get it out of the way. As I was cleaning I ran across a beautiful card. The top read: *To Someone Special on Mother's Day.*

It had a picture of a bistro set in a garden with a heart separately off to the side. Just below the picture there was a poem by Emily Matthews. It read:

**YOU HAVE SUCH A GIFT FOR CARING**
By Emily Matthews
Some people have a gift
for making life a little brighter,
for sharing someone's burdens,
and for making loads seem lighter,
For lifting someone's spirits
with a gentle word or two,
That suddenly can seem
to turn the grayest sky to blue....

Inside left:

For being there
at lonely times
to simply hold a hand
Or give a hug that says, "I care
and want to understand."
Some people have a gift-
A special blessing from above-
That makes the world
more beautiful
And fills it with
God's love.

Inside right:

My heart is so thankful
whenever I think
of the warm, caring things
that you do,
And I want you to know
Just how grateful I am
God makes wonderful people
Like you!
Happy Mother's Day

At the bottom in Zach's own writing he wrote:

*Thanks for always being a good Mother.*

*Love Zach*

Thanks Zach. I'll read this card each Mother's Day and know you are smiling down at me. I love you baby.


February 23, 2009

I was talking to Monica on the phone today. She had been watching wrestling with her husband Bill this past Monday night. Zach used to watch wrestling too. Zach would be amused when Monica talked about wrestling to him. She was such a nerd and it was so out of character.

Monica was studying while watching the wrestling. She looked up at the TV and someone in the audience was holding a sign that read: **"ZACH"**. That's all it said. She didn't really think much about it and went back to studying. When she looked up again, she saw a sign that said, "**HI MOM**".

I always call the kids on their birthdays. Monica's birthday was a few days later. I can't help but wonder if that happened on purpose.

Philippians 1:3 (kjv) *"I thank my God upon every remembrance of you"*[9]

**Kayla's Toast**

The month of December was hard. It had been a year since Zach passed away. I was trying to do my Christmas shopping but everything I saw I would think 'Oh Zach would like that, or He sure could have used this.' My niece Kayla and nephew Chris each called me on the anniversary of Zach's death. They both live in North Carolina so I had not been able to share a lot of the things that had happened in the past year. I told Kayla that I was still getting a lot of signs and looked forward to sharing them with her during Christmas. She said she had something to show me too.

She told me that she and some friends were at a bonfire during the week of Thanksgiving. She was thinking a lot about Zach's last Thanksgiving. She knew he had no idea that it would be his last and only had a week to live. Kayla had a drink in her hand so she poured some of it on the fire and said, "Here's to you Zach. I love you and miss you buddy." Kayla's friend took a picture of her with her cell phone as she toasted Zach. When she looked at the picture the letters Z A C were spelled out in smoke perfectly above the fire, in monogram style. It was in mirror form on Kayla's side but from the camera it was spelled normally. She gave me a copy of the picture when we got together at Christmas. There is no doubt it spells ZAC.

It never fails. It seems like when I'm starting to go through the unbearable pain of losing my son, God always does something for me or sends someone in my path to remind me that HE is in control and all is well.

## RAYBO

Several months ago, Karen lost her brother, Raybo to cancer. He was in his early 40s. I didn't know Karen very well at the time but I kept feeling like I should write her mom a letter. As usual the busyness of my life kept getting in the way and months passed and I still had not written the letter.

One morning I woke up and the thought of Karen's mother was heavy on my mind. I started praying for her. Later that morning I saw Karen and asked how her mom was doing. She said, "not too well". Her mother has started drinking a lot since her brother passed away. It had gotten so bad they had to put her in the hospital. Karen was leaving the next day to spend Christmas with her mom and the rest of the family. Everyone in her family lives in Tennessee except her.

I felt so badly that I had not written to her mom so I went home and started writing. I told her about some of the amazing signs I had received since Zach's death and even enclosed a copy of the cloud picture of the hand and Zach's name above his grave.

I explained how the devil pushes us to confusion and makes us feel like everything is our fault. If God had not planned for Raybo to go to Heaven, he may have suffered some type of physical disability for the rest of his life. Or he may have suffered more than she as a mother could bear to watch. I assured her there is a reason for all this. We may not realize it right now but God has our best interest in mind. Philippians 1:6 (niv) says *"being confident of this, that he who began a good work in you will carry it on to completion."*

Below is part of the letter I wrote to Karen's mom and dad:

*Tony Dungy lost his son just after Thanksgiving 2005. He gave a speech at a Super Bowl breakfast in February 2006 about his son. He told the story of a question asked of him by a very close friend. He asked Tony, "If you had a chance to bring your son back to earth with all that you know about Heaven. Would you?" I know what my answer is. No, I would not. Sure, I miss Zach. But I KNOW I will see him again someday and we will experience total happiness for eternity. God promised that. We can't let the devil win and turn us away from God. That would keep us from seeing our sons again. We should get closer to God instead. God gives us little rewards, showing us that our sons are happy if we just stop looking inward at our hurts and look outward to God. Talk to Him.*

*I have received so many signs from God that Zach is in Heaven. So many, that I plan to write a book about them. The signs included actions of birds, clouds that were shaped like a heart, a cross, the word "hi", and several other shapes in the clouds, just to name a few. I was able to take a picture of one of the cloud shapes which I have included. It was the letters "Zac" over my son's grave. It looks like a hand coming out of the clouds with the finger writing the "Z". God did this for me as a reward for "Trusting Him". God wants to reward you too, but you have to start moving forward and Trust Him.*

*John 9:3b (niv) ... "this happened so that the work of God might be displayed in his life."*

*Grief is actually a selfish emotion. (Why did this happen to me, I'm going to miss him, I hurt.....) Grief is necessary, but if it consumes you it will destroy you. You have to focus on where Raybo is at now and how happy he is. He is experiencing greater happiness than he could ever have here on this earth. Don't let his death destroy you. Fix your eyes on things above and you will get through it. It won't be easy. Someday, you'll be back together with him and Raybo will show **you** how to ride on the backs of whales!"*

I gave the six page letter to Karen later that day including the picture of the hand over my son's grave. I told her to read it too if she would like. I included a copy of the book "**Heaven**" as well as the condensed sixty page booklet.

A few weeks later I saw Karen. She came running up to me and gave me a huge hug. She said that my letter had changed her entire family's life. They all read it and have started going to church. Her mother stopped drinking and the family has started spending time together again. She said her mom showed my letter to her pastor and he read it in front of the whole church one Sunday morning. Her mom keeps the letter with her all the time and reads it constantly. Not a day has gone by that she has not read the letter.

What Karen said next has really stuck with me. She said, "Kim, I know that Zach's death was a horrible thing to experience but God is using his death to help others. You are being very faithful to carry his message to people in the same situation. You are changing lives. Thank you."

I understand now. I'm not going to let my son die in vain. I am going to keep running to everyone who comes across my path who has lost a loved one. God is real and He has been so faithful to show me this in unusual ways.

Romans 8:8-9 (niv) *"those controlled by the sinful nature cannot please God. You, however, are controlled not by the sinful nature but by the Spirit, if the Spirit of God lives in you."*

John 13:7 (niv) *"Jesus replied, "you do not realize now what I am doing, but later you will understand."*

## **GRIEF**

It is said that God never gives us more than we can handle. The biggest fear of my life was the thought of losing a child. I was sure that I would not be able to recover should it ever happen to me. Well, my worst fear happened. But God has totally blown my mind away with His Love and Faithfulness regarding my loss. He asked me to trust Him. I told him I would and I did.

This has been a riveting ordeal in many ways with many extremes. It has changed the way I look at everything. When you go through your toughest trial, it makes you realize you can handle anything, that there's nothing else to be afraid of.

Isaiah 40:31 (niv) *"Those who wait on the Lord will gain new strength; they will mount up with wings like eagles. They will run and not get tired. They will walk and not become weary."*

Jeremiah 9:24 (niv) *"but let him who boasts boast about this: that he understands and knows me, that I am the Lord, who exercises kindness, justice, and righteousness on earth, for in these I delight" declares the Lord."*

If you ever stop to think about it, Grief *is* such a selfish emotion. Your thoughts are:

- Why did this happen to me?
- I'm going to miss them

- I feel guilty
- I hurt so badly
- I'm never going to hug them again
- I'm not going to be able to go to his wedding
- He never gave me grandchildren

Have you ever thought about it? Grief is a necessary emotion but if you let it continue for too long, it can eat you up. You have to move forward. Your loved one wouldn't want you to hurt so much. And if they had accepted Christ they are happier than we will ever imagine while here on this earth!

**THOUGHTS**

People often ask WHY good people die young. Why doesn't God keep the good people around and let the bad ones die? I think I may know the answer. When a young person dies, we notice it more. We feel badly the person did not live a full life. They missed out on the wonderful milestones such as getting married, having children, and other similar events.

John 9:3b (niv) *"but this happened so that the work of God might be displayed in his life."*

We do not give God credit nor do we thank Him like we should when good things happen. Most times we don't recognize when we've received a blessing. We take it for granted. We remember and learn more readily from painful experiences. When we face painful experiences, we tend to seek God and answers with more emotion.

You will go to heaven if you have accepted Christ into your heart. Heaven is your reward not a punishment. What better place to be? You never have to worry about bills or sickness. There is no crime, no heartache, nothing bad to experience. Beauty is all around.

My guess is that a "bad" person doesn't die young so that they have a chance to accept Christ. When a person is "bad" it seems obvious they haven't done so. Wouldn't you agree? You can't do bad things and have Jesus in your heart.

Then there is the question why live for God all your life when you can be saved at the last minute and still go to Heaven. People think this is unfair. Why do good things and live a life that pleases God if the reward is the same in the end? Most people don't understand that the reward *is* different for each person.

Randy Alcorn explained it perfectly in his book **HEAVEN**. He explains that we face two judgments after we die. The first is "judgment of faith" and the second is "judgment of works".

"Judgment of faith" occurs when we die. It determines whether we go to Heaven or Hell. Salvation is a free gift from God. It is unconditional. All we have to do is accept this free gift. (Ephesians 2:8-9; Titus 3:5)

"Judgment of works" occurs when we stand before God and give an account of our lives. This is when we get the rewards for all that we've done for God's glory. As Randy Alcorn put it, "Rewards are conditional, dependent on our faithfulness. (2 Timothy 2:12, Revelation 2:26-28, 3:21)"[10]

We don't know when our time on earth will be up which is another reason not to delay accepting Christ into our hearts. I assure you my son had no idea he would never come home again the night he died. There are no guarantees that we have the next five minutes to live.

Several things became clear:

- When I wondered if Zach was good enough to go to Heaven, God showed me blood running from a picture of Zach's tattoo of praying hands. It reminded me of John 3:16 (niv) *"For God so loved the world that he gave his one and only Son that whoever BELIEVES in him shall not perish but have eternal life"*. I know Zach believed in God. Jesus took care of the rest of it for him.
- God does not put conditions on His love for us. He loves us no matter what. He wants us to go to heaven. But he still gives us "free will". It's up to us to make the final choice to go there.
- Each day is a gift. We don't know which moment is our last. Don't have any regrets. Make the best of EVERY Moment.
- Each person you meet has a need. It may just be the need for a hug or a kind word. Don't let the moment pass without encouraging each person you meet. I was surprised at how people yelled and screamed at Haven and her dad when they left the hospital after the news of Zach's death as they drove home in a daze.

- <u>Read your bible.</u> When I was at my worst, all God wanted me to do was TRUST HIM. Deut.13:3,4(niv) *"The Lord your God is testing you to see if you truly*

*love him with all your heart and soul. Serve only the Lord your God and fear him alone. Obey His commands, listen to his voice and cling to him".*
- Isaiah 25:8-9 (niv) *"he will swallow up death forever, The Sovereign Lord will wipe away the tears from all faces; he will remove the disgrace of his people from all the earth. The Lord has spoken. In that day they will say, 'Surely this is our God; we trusted in him and he saved us. This is the Lord, we trusted in him: let us rejoice and be glad in his salvation'".*
- Isaiah 40:5 (niv) *"And the glory of the Lord will be revealed, and all mankind together will see it. For the mouth of the Lord has spoken."*
- Isaiah 40:26 (niv) *"Lift your eyes and look to the heavens, who created all these? He who brings out the starry host one by one, and calls them each by name. Because of his great power and mighty strength not one of them is missing".*
- Isaiah 40:31(niv) *"But those who hope in the Lord will renew their strength. They will soar on wings like eagles; they will run and not grow weary, they will walk and not be faint."*
- Jeremiah 33:3 (niv) *" Call to me and I will answer you and tell you great and unsearchable things you do not know."*
- John 9:3 (niv) *"Neither this man nor his parents sinned, said Jesus, but this happened so that the work of God might be displayed in his life".*

- Acts20:22-24 (niv) *"And now compelled by the Spirit, I am going to Jerusalem, not knowing what will happen to me there. I only know that in every city the Holy Spirit warns me that prison and hardships are facing me. However, I consider my life worth nothing to me, if only I may finish the race and complete the task the Lord Jesus has given me-the task of testifying to the gospel of God's grace."*

So HOW can you be sure you will go to Heaven? It's really simple. Jesus did the hard part.

1. **Turn away from your sins**.
   Mark 1:15 (paraphrased) Acknowledge your sins and change the direction of your life.
   Acts 26:18 (paraphrased) open your eyes and turn from darkness to light, and from the power of Satan to God, so you may receive forgiveness of your sins and receive a place among God's people, who are set apart by faith in me.
2. **Believe in Jesus Christ and Receive him into your life**. You have to believe that Jesus died on the cross in order for your sins to be forgiven. Then ask Him into your life to help you do the right thing, make decisions regarding your life that pleases Him. Revelation 3:20 (nlt) "Jesus said, 'Look! Here I stand at the door and knock. If you hear me calling and open the door, I will come in,

and we will share a meal as friends.'"[11] Don't think you have to 'clean up' your life *before* you ask Jesus into your heart. He takes us just as we are. The past is wiped clean once we ask him into our heart.

Faith is described best in the book of Hebrews. Hebrews 11:1 (niv) "Now faith is being sure of what we hope for and certain of what we do not see." Hebrews chapter eleven describes a lot of events listed in the bible where people had faith in God and how he rewards them for trusting him.

A relationship with Jesus Christ is very much like parents and their children here on earth. Children are very trusting with their parents. Parents provide for them, teach them, and love them no matter what the circumstances. As parents we try to guide our children by telling them no. You warn them not to touch a hot stove. Some children are disobedient and touch the stove anyway. They learn very quickly not to ever do it again. It hurts you to see them suffer but it is for their own good. This is how our heavenly father is with us. He will let us keep going in the same direction until something happens to make us realize we don't ever want to go that way again. It's called free will. He allows us to make our own choices. When we choose to live outside of God's boundaries, we chose to live outside of his protection.

God speaks to us in many ways. Sometimes he speaks to us in dreams like He did with Joseph in Genesis 37, or with an audible voice as with Moses in Exodus 3, or through a burden on your heart where something is bothering you, or nudging you as described in Nehemiah 2. Listen to Him. He loves you and wants to take care of you.

I've trusted God with my life. He has been and *is* my best friend. When the worst thing imaginable happened to me, losing one of my children, He was *very* faithful to show me He was still there. His promises are real. I urge you to get to know Him. He will bless you and surprise you beyond anything you could ever imagine.

**In Loving Memory .......**

People who passed away within the first year

1. Denny  3/28/90 - 9/15/08
2. Marilyn  1/26/28 – 10/13/07
3. Neal  10/24/60 – 1/10/08
4. Raybo  7/28/66 - 8/5/08
5. Gene  4/5/36 - 1/26/08
6. Mike  1/11/54 - 2/25/08
7. Ciera  1/30/06 - 3/10/08
8. Bill  8/20/47 - 3/18/08
9. Jane  January 2008
10. Pete  5/9/08
11. Katherine  7/14  - 8/11/08
12. Grandma Cruise  10/22/22 - 8/29/08
13. Grandma Marion  5/5/12 – 2/6/08
14. Devin  June 2008
15. Manny  May 2008
16. Katlynn  9/13/07 – 9/22/07
17. Tommy  May 2008

**<u>Also in Loving Memory of:</u>**
Brian Gaetano  5/27/83 – 2/10/07
Sean Thurston  7/8/83 – 10/22/06


His heart grieves even more for you, Let God have his moments to take care of you.

[1] You may read more about these experiences and God's faithfulness in my book, "HE SPEAKS".

[2] *90 Minutes in Heaven* Don Piper & Cecil Murphey Copyright

[3] Tony Dungy Super Bowl Breakfast speech 2006 All Rights Reserved

[4] The Message, BibleGateway.com Copyright 1993, 1994,1995,1996,2000,2001,2002 by Eugene H. Peterson All Rights Reserved

[5] *Holy Bible (NIV) Life Application Bible* copyright 1973, 1978, 1984,by International Bible Society, used by permission of Zondervan Publishing House and Tyndale House Publishers page 198 All Rights Reserved

[6] *Holy Bible (NIV) Life Application Bible* copyright 1973, 1978, 1984,by International Bible Society, used by permission of Zondervan Publishing House and Tyndale House Publishers page 485 All Rights Reserved

[7] *The Power of Praying*, pg 68, Stormie Omartian copyright 1995-2009 Published by Muze, Inc. All Rights Reserved

[8] *Holy Bible (NIV) Life Application Bible* copyright 1973, 1978, 1984,by International Bible Society, used by permission of Zondervan Publishing House and Tyndale House Publishers page 917 All Rights Reserved

[9] Holy Bible King James Version All Rights Reserved

[10] Heaven by Randy Alcorn, Page 47 copyright 2004 All Rights Reserved by Eternal Perspective Ministries www.epm.org, www.randyalcorn.blogspot.com

[11] *New Living Translation Holy Bible* All Rights Reserved